wish i

could

have

said

goodbye

SHARI A. BRADY

To Becky,
Soooo glad to
be friends! You're the best.
Love,
Shari

2/13

Summary: While sixteen-year-old Carmella comes to terms with her older
sister's death, she finds the strength to overcome the consequences of co-
dependency and the courage to fall in love for the first time.

[1. Grief – Fiction 2. Death – Fiction 3. Sisters – Fiction
Co-dependency – Fiction 4. Family problems 5. Chicago] 1. Title

For Jane

November 26, 1955 – September 7, 1992

Even in the darkest night, I can still see your light.

Chapter 1

I hug Francesca's purse tight against my chest and rest my head against the corner of my closet. This is me since my big sister died four weeks ago. Francesca was six years older than me, and at twenty-three she became one of those people you read about in the tabloids, only she wasn't an actor in Hollywood. She was my big sister who accidentally overdosed at her own party and now she's not here to help me get over the fact I let her down, or to give me one reason why I should keep on living since my universe exploded and turned to dust.

I close my eyes and make a list, the kind Francesca and I would make when the lights were out and we were supposed to be sleeping.

Why I should live the rest of my life in my closet

1. I don't have to talk to anyone.
2. I don't have to listen to Mom and Dad fight.
3. I don't have to face the rest of my life without my big sister.

Francesca and I had a pact to keep the lists just between us and we swore each other to secrecy before we made our first one. When Francesca went to college and was home for a break or a visit, we didn't make many lists. And then when she graduated, the lists stopped. I forgot about the lists until I found one in her purse the night she died. It was her Monday to do list.

"Carmella?" My mother taps on the door. "Could you—?"

I slide the closet door open and squint up at my mother.

"We need you to come out. Your father's got his coat on. He's waiting."

"I'm not going."

"Carmella, don't do this." She pushes up the sleeves of her burnt orange pullover and folds her arms in front of her. "We need you."

I want to tell Mom I can't reduce my big sister's life to twelve boxes and stuff them underneath the steps of my parents' basement. But I won't say what I'm thinking. I don't want to make things worse for her and Dad.

My mother's eyes are a million miles away. They've been like that ever since we got the news. "I know this is hard, Carmella, but Father Carlucci says packing up her things and moving her out of the apartment will help us start to heal."

"What if I don't want to move her things out of there? I want everything to stay the same."

"Please, I don't have the energy to fight." Mom's hair is tucked behind her ears, all messy, and her make up is rubbed off of her puffy eyes.

"Fine." I set Francesca's purse down on top of my red Converse shoes and drag myself towards the steps.

When I get into the kitchen, Mom hands me my coat.

My father's pacing in front of the sink, crunching on corn chips. The veins in the side of his head pop out while he chews.

Mom grabs her purse from the scratched up wooden kitchen table they always talk about replacing, but never do.

"The owners from Lincoln Distributors sent flowers to the office Friday. How did they find out?" she asks.

My father stops in front of the door and rubs his forehead with his left hand. "I don't know. Obviously, someone at the office told them. We never should have let the truth get past the family."

"What are you talking about?" Mom squeezes the strap of her black leather purse tight.

"Yesterday, Mary at Davenport Motor Works asked what happened to Francesca. I told her she died of a fatal arrhythmia. From here on in, if anyone asks, that's the story. And when you go back to school, you tell everyone the same thing." He points to me.

"But most of them know what happened." I zip my jacket.

"Not all of them. Tell Anna and your other friends to keep quiet too."

Dad doesn't know I haven't spoken to anyone but Anna in the last year. My only friends lately were Francesca and Donny. Mom and Dad don't know much about me at all now. When Francesca started having problems in middle school, I disappeared.

"You lied? You told a customer our daughter died from a fatal heart condition?" Mom swipes her hair behind her ear.

"Gina, our daughter died at a party where kids were doing drugs. People see that as a reflection on us. Since my father passed away and I took over the business two years ago, I've been working my ass off. I don't want anything to jeopardize our reputation and I don't want all my hard work to go to hell."

My mother's eyes glass over, her face drops like all her muscles turned into water and poured out. "Joe, this is our daughter. How can you talk like this? People will understand. It was an accident."

"This type of shit only happens to kids who are on drugs. Francesca was in the wrong place at the wrong time, that's all. If she didn't move in with that asshole Donny, she'd be alive right now." My father stabs his finger in the air.

"I don't believe this. So when I talk to people at work, I'm supposed to *lie* about how my daughter died?" My mother's eyes glass over.

"Say it was a heart thing and you don't want to talk about it. People won't push. And that goes for you too." My dad plucks his keys out of his coat pocket. "Let's go."

***

The three of us head up the creaky steps to Donny and Francesca's third floor apartment. We had to walk two blocks struggling to hold onto the flattened boxes and packing tape. Parking on city streets is always a pain, especially on Saturdays when everyone is home from work. Most people work Monday through Friday in this neighborhood, except for Francesca and Donny.

Donny works weekends at the bar down the street. That's how they got this apartment. A year ago, Donny met a guy who was transferred to China for a four-year assignment and needed to rent out his top floor condo in a cool brownstone building. Francesca was so excited; she thought they got lucky. The place was only a few blocks from the famous Second City Theatre in Chicago. Francesca thought she was going to move in here and get her life back on track.

Francesca worked at different restaurants for a while, but last summer she didn't work at all. Around middle of August, she stopped returning my calls. When she finally called me back it was the first week in September to ask me to go to an AA meeting with her. It was a week before she died and the last time I ever heard her voice.

Dad sets his stack of boxes down and knocks. Mom starts to cry. She pulls a tissue out of her purse. She hands one to me, but I'm not gonna cry. I'm gonna be strong for Mom and Dad because that's what families do for each other.

Donny opens the door and we get a whiff of rotten food like moldy cheese. We haven't seen him since the funeral.

"Hi," Donny says. He combs his messy dishwater blond hair with his fingers, like he just woke up. His green T-shirt is all wrinkled.

"C'mon in." He steps back and holds out his hand. "Hey, sis." He smiles.

"Hi." I almost walk towards the kitchen, but I stop myself. Francesca loved to cook. I kept her company in the kitchen while she made stuff. They were always broke, so she cooked a lot of pasta.

Everywhere I look I see Francesca. Like her favorite fake painting of a sunrise on the beach she bought from a guy on the street for ten bucks when she first moved in with Donny. Francesca and I dreamed of living near the ocean, where the air is always warm and people are more relaxed. She was sure the painting meant good luck for her. I run my finger along the tacky gold frame.

"We were supposed to be awesome career women, get married, have kids and live next door to each other, two blocks from the beach," I whisper. "That was our plan."

I remember thinking how much I liked Donny and was so happy for Francesca. We were both sure her life was going to finally get better.

Donny leads us into the bedroom.

He points to the closet. "I boxed up her shoes, just the hanging stuff needs to be done."

I think I might puke. I push past my parents, who are stiff like statues. I run straight to the bathroom where Francesca and I hung out when we wanted to talk in secret. I close and lock the door, taking my usual seat on the side of the tub, staring at the toilet where Francesca parked her foot as she blew cigarette smoke out the tiny frosted paned window. I rock back and forth and howl into my sleeve.

I bend down and run my fingers across the tiny tiles on the floor. I imagine her lying here, taking her last breaths, all alone. I grab my chest. I wish she hadn't died in here alone. I wish I could have been with her, to hold her hand or to hug her. I wish I could have said goodbye.

"Carmella." My mother knocks on the door. "Are you okay?"

I stand up and turn the cold water on full blast. "I'm fine," my voice cracks. I clear my throat. "I'll be right out."

I open the door, and I hear Dad shout. "How can you live with yourself? This is all your fault."

"Don't go blaming me. All I did was try and love her," Donny stomps out of the apartment, the door slamming behind him.

I walk into the bedroom. My father is mumbling over the high-pitched scream of the packing tape as he seals the top of a box.

Mom sniffles as she takes Francesca's clothes off the hangers, folds them and puts them carefully in the box on the floor next to her.

Dad stands in the middle of the room, staring at the dresser, the tape dispenser dangling from his right hand.

"Where's Donny?" I ask.

Mom turns towards me. "He left. He shouldn't be here." She folds Francesca's blue and white plaid shirt.

"Wait," I say. "Can I have that one?"

Mom clutches the shirt. "This old thing? Why would you want this?"

"Because. It was her favorite."

Mom passes me the shirt. "Okay." She shakes her head.

Holding it up to my nose, I smell Francesca and for a tiny fraction of a second, I get her back.

I put the shirt down next to my purse on the bed. "What should I do?"

Dad hands me a small box. "Donny says there's a few things out there."

I take the box from him and walk into the kitchen, pretending she'll be standing at the sink, excited to see me as usual, throwing her arms around me in one of her over-the-top hugs.

I turn my head. There's a small magnet on the side of the fridge in the shape of an old potbelly stove with red letters that say "Francesca's Kitchen" across the belly. Donny bought it for her and she loved the stupid thing. I shove the magnet into my pocket.

***

I stretch my red and white tiny-flowered comforter over my crossed legs and try not to look over at Francesca's empty bed, still made up with the matching bedspread. My guitar sits in the stand and stares at me like an abandoned dog. I haven't been able to go near it since we got the call. Francesca talked my parents into giving me the guitar for my eighth grade graduation, a gift from all three of them. It's the same style of acoustic guitar John Lennon had. She knew I'd go ballistic over it. I used a black Sharpie marker to copy his famous character sketch, just like the one he had on the guitar he used during the Bed-In for Peace. My parents had a fit when they saw the drawing. They thought I'd ruined the guitar.

I tried to explain how much I admired John Lennon, how I want to be an artist who changes the world like he did. In the middle of my explanation, the phone rang. The office called with an emergency. We were supposed to finish talking later, but never did.

I was playing "Imagine" when my mother stormed through the door screaming that Francesca was dead. Then she fainted.

I glance over at Francesca's empty bed and turn out the light. Staring at the moon outside my window, missing Francesca so bad I want to curl up and die, I wonder how Donny's surviving.

I close my eyes. A replay of the day flashes through my head. I start to drift into the still black waters of the night.

Then I smell cigarette smoke.

I see Francesca in her bathroom, standing with her foot on the toilet, blowing smoke out the window, making fun of all our goofy distant relatives that were at her wake and funeral.

I'm sitting on the side of the tub, laughing.

Francesca smiles at me, taking a long drag from her cigarette. Then she tells me she's okay.

My eyes fly open.

I sit up.

My heart jumps into my throat. I grab for the lamp and miss. My water glass falls onto the carpet. I reach for the lamp again and turn it on. I stare at the end of my bed. No Francesca. I fly out of bed. I blink, rub my sweaty forehead and look around the room. My legs shake as I crawl back into bed.

The cigarette smoke chokes me.

I scream but nothing comes out.

Chapter 2

Reasons why wearing a uniform to school should be outlawed

1. If your big sister dies, you should be allowed to wear all black forever.
2. When you dress like everyone else at Trinity High School, and you're an outcast, you're living a lie.
3. A uniform covers up people's real personalities.
4. Wearing plaid every day for several years of your life is bound to result in bad things happening to your sense of fashion.

The last period bell rings, but I'm already out in the parking lot. I ditched my last class. Today was my first day back after missing four weeks, and I couldn't take the "sorry for your loss" blah blah blah of the teachers and the kids looking at me like I'm a total freak show because my sister died, so I went to the nurse and lied. I told her I felt sick to my stomach and had my period.

She directed me to sit down in the blue vinyl hospitalesque-looking chair next to her desk, pulled out the thermometer and stuck it under my tongue.

"Oh dear, so awful," she said. "So young for this, so unfair to endure this kind of loss *and* be that time of the month."

With sad, pathetic eyes, she handed me a can of ginger ale and excused me from my last class. I headed straight outside to the ginormous elm tree next to the parking lot where I could hang out and doodle until the last bell. I blink to try and clear the fuzz from my eyes.

I wish I could put toothpicks in my eyes to keep my lids open like Fred Flintstone, because I'm so tired and I can't let myself fall asleep. I have to keep my eye on the doors so I can spot Anna right away. She'll never notice me here and I don't want her to freak out thinking something happened to me. She's been recruited by my parents to drive me to work at the bakery like I'm a complete imbecile, since Mom and Dad are so paranoid something will happen to me, they won't let me drive. Mom will pick me up after work and drive me home, then go back to the office for a few more hours. Not sure how long I'll be driven everywhere like a two-year-old, but I pray this overprotective craziness ends soon.

I also hate having to get back to my life, back to school and the bakery, carrying on as though tragedy hasn't struck me like a pianist hitting a bad note in the middle of her first concert in Carnegie Hall. Wearing my usual green and blue plaid uniform skirt is wrong, as if everything's back to normal now, when in fact, nothing is normal. Before the Francesca shock, I wrote songs. Sappy songs, serious songs. Lyrics popped into my head during math class or earth science and I'd write them down. Now all I do is make lists. I've seen my big sister standing at the end of my bed for the last three nights and I miss her so bad I don't think I'll ever laugh again.

Chewing on my pen, I spot Anna, so I walk over to her hand-me-down white Chevy Cavalier that's been through her three older sisters. I think it's a little unfair Anna has three sisters and the only one I had got taken from me. Not that I wish one of Anna's sisters would die, but if I were God, I wouldn't snatch someone's *only* sister away.

I dread the thought of going into work, facing Mrs. Sparacini and the regular customers who know the truth of what happened to Francesca and might treat me like I'm a freak. My sister died of a drug overdose and for some reason that seems to make her death different. I overheard people at the wake whispering about how it is such a waste when a young person's death is so preventable. Not that I wish Francesca had cancer or was in a car accident, but if she died like that, people wouldn't blame her, as if she made a bad decision and death happened to be the outcome. They'd feel sorry for her— not sorry for her life. Maybe Dad's right about hiding the truth.

Anna waves from two rows down, her straight long blond hair tucked behind the oversized ears she hates. I'd trade her Irish stick figure with oversized ears for my oversized Italian thighs any day.

She gives me a gentle hug like I'm a china doll then gives me a once over. "Mello, you okay? You look like shit." Anna throws her bag in the back.

We slide into the car. I pull my heavy bag in with me.

"Thanks, way to pump me up, total ego boost."

"Sorry. You look exhausted. Are you sleeping at all?"

I shake my head and pull my hair tie out to redo my ponytail. My hair needs smoothing before work.

"You wanna go hang out at the mall this weekend? I miss searching through the sale racks with you all day."

I shrug my shoulders. I'd rather spend the weekend curled up in my bed under my comforter, or sitting in the corner of my closet.

She fiddles with the car stereo. "C'mon, what'd you think?"

"I'm thinking no," I say.

As usual, I pretend to like Anna's country music. She has no idea I secretly cringe whenever I hear the twangy voices and slide guitars. I know how the music puts her in a good mood, so I've never told her the truth.

Anna brushes her long blond hair. "Maybe you should skip work."

Maybe she's right. I'm so not in the mood. But then I think about my alternative. Go home, sit on my bed and stare at a guitar that totally gives me the creeps.

"I can't. I don't want to let Mrs. Sparacini down. It's only a few hours. I'll survive."

***

Anna pulls up to the bakery and stops the car.

"Thanks again, Anna."

Anna's eyebrows fly up into the air and she looks like she's got a cartoon bubble with a light bulb floating above her head. "Wait, I wanna go in," she says. "You've been workin' here for six months and I've never brought anything home for my dad. He's got a wicked sweet tooth and my parents told us last night he landed another promotion at work. He'll be VP *and* CIO of a new division of Boeing now." Anna drives to the back of the building, and parks in the lot. "How awesome is that?"

"Yeah," I say.

I imagine Anna's family having some happy-as-the-Brady-Bunch dinner tonight. I'll go home and throw leftovers in the microwave and eat dinner on the couch in the family room watching cable reruns of the *Dick Van Dyke Show*, or *I Love Lucy*, not because

I like those stupid shows, but because the laugh track makes me forget I'm all alone.

***

Walking into Il Mulano Bakery is like walking into heaven. The smell of fresh baked bread, vanilla icing, chocolate, homemade cannoli, cookies, cake, wraps me up in a warm blanket of yum. Mrs. Sparacini always puts aside a treat for me to eat before I start work, like some kind of filled pastry or butter cookies. I'm not in the mood to eat so I'll give my treat to Anna.

The bell on the door jingles and Mrs. Sparacini races out from the back. "Carmella, honey." She runs up to me, grabs me, and squeezes me tight, like she did at Francesca's wake. Mrs. Sparacini isn't skinny like Mom and Aunt Maria. Her hugs are like her bakery, big and warm. And she puts tons of energy into everything she does—even a hug.

Mrs. Sparacini finally lets me come up for air. Anna's scanning the cases filled with cookies, cakes, biscotti and tiramisu. Only three loaves of bread sit perched on the shelf, which is normal for this time of day. Mrs. Sparacini sells almost all of her bread and filled rolls first thing in the morning to her regular customers.

Anna turns around. "Mmm ... Mello, how do you work here? Everything looks and smells like ..."

"Heaven." I head towards the back room. "Just yell when you decide."

Mrs. Sparacini follows, talking behind me. "I have three boxes of supplies for you to put away and I put a cannoli on the work table. I know cannolis are your favorite so make sure to eat it. You need to keep up your strength." She turns around and smiles, her giant brown eyes filled with warmth.

"And don't forget, this Saturday is the big Lombardo wedding, so you need to be here by six thirty in the morning to work the register." She disappears into her office.

"Yep." I pull my jeans out of my bag, get my white apron and go change. Something about getting out of my uniform and being here in the bakery makes me feel a little better.

When I come back, I sneak the cannoli into a box for Anna. I haven't been able to eat much lately and I'm tired of everyone telling me I'm going to get sick or starve to death. I get a drink of water from the sink. The bell jingles on the front door.

I swallow and yell, "I got it."

People come from suburbs all around the Chicago area just so Mrs. Sparacini can make them one of her cakes. This is a quiet time of day for the bakery so she likes me to take care of customers so she can catch up on paperwork. When there aren't any customers in the bakery, I put stuff away in the back. I'd love to learn how to decorate cakes like Mrs. Sparacini, but I've never told her. I'm sure if I did, she wouldn't take me seriously, so what's the point?

I push the swinging door open and Anna turns around as the two cutest guys in the entire world walk in. Tying my apron, I walk towards the counter. Anna's eyes fall out of her skull.

"Can I help you?" I wipe my face, imagining I've got MY SISTER IS DEAD written all over it.

"We're looking for Mrs. Sparacini," the tall dimpled guy says. His hair is cut just above his eyebrows, his jaw squared-off like he's some model or something. I wonder how God doles out dimples.

"Oh, sure. One second. You decide what you want yet?" I ask Anna.

She glances over at them, then back at me. "Hmm. Can't decide. The more time I spend in this place, the better things get." Anna puffs her chest out and smiles.

I'm sure my face turned a bright shade of purple, blue or pink. Or maybe chalk-white like all the blood has rushed out of my body.

Anna's fearless flirting catches me off guard. I spin around, my head down. "I'll go get Mrs. Sparacini."

I walk into her office. "There are a couple of guys out front to see you."

Mrs. Sparacini peers over her half-glasses, her old chair squeaks. "What guys?"

She stretches her neck squinting at the calendar on the wall. "Oh, right, completely forgot." She holds her hand up to her forehead, smashing down her salt and pepper hair.

"They're here to order a birthday cake for a little boy. I guess he's pretty sick. Tell them I'll be right out."

I nod.

I hear Anna flirting as I approach the door. This can only mean one thing: She's struck up a conversation and I'll be forced to actually speak to them.

I push the door open to the front, and rush straight for the cash register. They all turn towards me.

"She'll be right out." I think I'm smiling. Can't tell what I'm doing from the shock of communicating with boys who don't totally gross me out.

"Thanks," cute short-haired guy says.

"Carmella. I'd like you to meet Jeremy and Howie." Anna holds her hands out like she's serving them up on platter.

I nod. "Grace to neat you. I mean, nice to meet you." *Ugh*

Jeremy, with a face like a model, turns to me. "Your friend Anna told us you're the cake decorator extraordinaire. You'd be helping Mrs. Sparacini decorate my little brother's cake?"

"Yep." I give Anna a look like *thanks for totally lying and making me talk to these strange guys.*

My voice cracks. I'm about to come clean about not being a cake decorator like Mrs. Sparacini, but who cares? Lying is so much easier than telling the truth and besides, I'll never see them again. I clear my throat, to try and dislodge the lump of fear stuck in it. I think I'm suddenly stricken with post-traumatic death disorder in the form of boy phobia.

Howie, who's wearing shorts in the middle of October in Chicago, steps up to the counter and puts his arm up on the register. "So how long have you been a cake artist?" He smiles at me, his dark eyes peeking through his wavy black hair. I'm dying to ask him if he wears shorts to show off his awesome legs or what, but I'm too chicken.

I've never had a totally hot guy flirt with me and never been called a cake artist.

"Cake artist?" I scratch my head. "About three months. I've only worked here for six." My head is so hot I imagine the hair tie around my pony melting. "So, what's the age, I mean, how old is Jeremy's little brother? Is he going to be okay?" I wonder what the hell is taking Mrs. Sparacini so long to come out here.

Jeremy leans on the bakery case laughing, flinging his hair, totally flirting with Anna like he's in another universe. He doesn't hear anything.

Howie jumps in. "Jeremy's bro is turning seven. He's better now, but he's been really sick since he was a kid. He told his parents all he wanted was a Star Wars Millennium Falcon cake so he could put C-3PO, R2D2 and Luke Skywalker on top of it. Jeremy plans all his little bro's birthday parties."

"Wow. What an awesome big brother." I grab a pen and an order form.

"Yeah, I think so. A lot of kids at school think it's weird how much Jeremy does for his brother, but I get it."

I nod. "Totally, me too."

Finally, Mrs. Sparacini comes walking in. "Which one of you handsome young men is Jeremy? Your mother and I spoke on the phone this morning, and I know exactly what to do. You have the photo?"

Jeremy hands Mrs. Sparacini a picture of some Star Wars ship. She passes it to me. "I see Carmella's already got the order started." She peeks over her half-glasses and smiles. "Bring the order form to my office when you're done and I'll staple it to my notes. This cake will be ready on Sunday around one."

Mrs. Sparacini shakes Jeremy's hand and walks away, pushing through the door.

I take down Jeremy's information, even though I know Mrs. Sparacini has his name and address on her notes but she likes things written down twice for two reasons: one, she might lose the information; and two, Mrs. Sparacini doesn't believe in computers. It's a moral issue for her. She thinks computers are the demise of our society.

As I double-check the order and paper clip the picture to the form, Howie, Jeremy and Anna chat each other up.

I pretend to be busy so I can avoid joining in on their conversation.

Howie says to Jeremy. "Dude, Anna plays volleyball."

Jeremy's face lights up. "Really? Me too."

Anna walks up to the register, leading them all over to me. She puts her hands on her hips. The three of them crowd around in front of me.

Anna flings her hair. "You surprised? You're thinkin' I'm too short but I'm not. I've got a wicked spike. Come check me out Friday night. Mello's gonna be there."

My eyes fly open and I drop my pen. I bend down and pick it up, catching Anna's eye. *What. The. Hell?* I'm not going.

Anna knows what I'm saying, but ignores it. She turns to Jeremy. "So?"

"You're on. What school you play at?" Jeremy asks.

"St. Peter's." Anna lifts her chin in the air. "Number two in our division. Friday's one of our biggest games of the season. We play our rivals."

"Private school division, huh," Jeremy says.

Howie turns to me. "Awesome. We'll meet you there."

Anna gives me a puppy dog pathetic look.

"Sure, yep." I squeeze the pen and put on my best Academy Award performance of *I'm so excited to be going to Anna's volleyball game with two dudes I don't know.* OMG. I can't handle this right now.

Jeremy pulls his phone out of his pocket. "So all I need is the time and the place."

Anna rattles off the details, smiling the whole time.

I'm ticked off Anna's pushed this on me when I'm trying to deal with Francesca.

"Sorry, but got to get back to work. Nice meeting you two." I spin around and walk through the multi-colored swinging door into the back room where the cake decorating station is and lean on the table, my arms folded. Anna's going to be royally disappointed when I tell her I'm not going, but there's no way.

I hear them laughing for a few seconds then Anna yells, "Mello. Yo! I gotta go."

Pushing through the door I know the boys are gone so I roll my eyes at Anna.

She lets out a laugh. "Over here. These things, whatever they are, I'll take six." Anna taps her finger on the glass. "Just throw them in a bag. I gotta run so I can study before dinner. I got a huge test in AP physics tomorrow. Oh my God! Did you see those two? What about that Jeremy dude? And Howie? This is like hitting the jackpot, Mello."

I reach into the case, and slide the pastries into the box with the cannoli I couldn't eat. "The name for these is sfogliatelle. They're a pastry filled with ricotta cheese and dried lemon zest. Your dad will love you for bringing these home."

"Mello. You're changing the subject. Aren't you psyched? We finally met a few guys who are new blood, who we haven't been hanging out with since pre-school."

As I tape the sides of the box I know I'm disappointing her, but I can't help it.

"I'm totally *not* in the mood to hang out with people. I just want to be alone. I can't go." I ring up the sfogliatelle.

Anna pulls her money out. "Mello, I'm not going to let you wallow. I didn't want to tell you this, but I had a talk with my parents last night and we decided the best thing for you was to not be alone this weekend. It's been over a month now and you need to get out. My parents said you should keep busy. They've experienced ..."

I slam the register closed.

I want to scream at her. *Death, Anna. Just say it,* but I can't.

"C'mon. I'm totally crazed about this Jeremy dude and this is completely selfish of me, but at the same time, you can't deny going to my game might end up being fun for you. Besides, when was the last time you came to cheer me on at one of my games?"

I take a deep breath. "Freshman year. But you don't understand. I can't go sit with two strangers. I can't handle it right now.

She picks up her box. "Then go with Hannah, Izzy and Madison."

"No way. They're total jock bitches. Teasing me about being a virgin? I swore I'd never speak to them again. They're your friends now, not mine."

Anna huffs. "You shouldn't let people get to you so easily, Mello. You're too sensitive. They were just teasing. Hannah and Izzy are virgins too. Look at me. I'm a virgin and proud of it."

I laugh a little, realizing Anna's right. This is important to her. I may feel like my world is shattered, but Anna's isn't and she deserves a chance with this Jeremy guy. Plus, Anna's been on the volleyball team *and* the basketball team since freshman year and I didn't go to any of her games last year.

"Okay. I'll go. I'll go and sit with the bitches I haven't spoken to in months and a couple of dudes we just met. But you owe me."

Anna jumps up, pumping her arm in the air. "Yes." She races towards the door, and swings it open. "You won't regret this. I'm sure this is exactly what you need right now. Catch you tomorrow." Anna flies out the door.

I walk into the kitchen to put some supplies away and make a list.

Worst scenario if I go to Anna's volleyball game

1. I get teased again for being a virgin.
2. I say something so stupid to Howie and Jeremy and they think I'm a loser.
3. I have to focus so hard on not making an ass out of myself that I forget to be sad about Francesca.

Chapter 3

Reasons why I want Francesca to keep visiting me at night

1. We have a new sister secret.
2. Maybe her visits mean she doesn't hate me for letting her down.
3. We should never, ever be separated.

I add four more tiny boxes to the twenty I drew in the margin of my Geometry notebook yesterday, then put my pencil down so Mr. Gilmore thinks I'm listening to his lecture. Thank God my desk is in the back of the room for this class. The only way to get through Geometry is by doodling and if I were in the front row, I'd be screwed.

When my three minutes of listening are up, I shade in the left side of all the boxes one by one and my eyes start to cross. It's so hard to stay awake today. I didn't sleep well again last night. Francesca showed up at the end of my bed, and then disappeared into the darkness. Day number two back to school has been brutal.

"Carmella!" Mr. Gilmore's voice scares the shit out of me. My head is on my desk. I must have fallen asleep. I lift my head up. Twenty pairs of eyes are staring at me like I'm a freak show.

The bell rings and I gather my stuff. As I walk to my next class, I think about the first time I found out Francesca was taking drugs. I was over at Francesca and Donny's place, about six months after they moved in together. They tried to hide what they were doing from me, but they seemed way too goofy after only a few beers so I asked them what was going on.

"Promise you won't tell Mom and Dad," Francesca said to me. "They will totally overreact, like they always do, especially Mom. Sister promise, okay?"

"I don't know," I said. I was scared. I didn't want Francesca to shut me out of her life.

"Think about all the kids with ADD who take drugs every day, or all the parents who take Prozac when they're stressed out to the max," Francesca said.

"Listen, sis. Google prescription drug use. Everyone's on somethin' now. Just don't drive on the downers and you're good to go," Donny said as he and Francesca high fived each other and laughed.

"Get that worried look off your face," Francesca said.

I knew Francesca was headed for disaster and I didn't do anything to try and stop it. I wonder how Donny is, and if he misses her as much as I do. I want to talk to him. I gotta convince Anna to drive me into the city and I think I know what to do.

***

The last period bell blasts. Mrs. Kamen, my French teacher, stands in front of her desk, dressed in her usual too-tight skirt and button-up powder blue silk blouse.

She shouts, "I've got the brochures about student exchange/study abroad opportunities we talked about last week, if anyone is interested. Remember, this is a fabulous opportunity to live in France for a semester. You'll learn about the culture and can take some classes in the culinary arts if you're interested. Traveling abroad always gives you a competitive edge on college applications, which you'll all be doing as seniors next year." She waves brochures in the air as she sits on the edge of the desk.

Mrs. Kamen gives me the 'sorry for you' look as I attempt to file out of the room. She stops me when I get close to her.

"Carmella, remember there are counselors here at school, if you need to talk," she says.

"Yep, thanks."

"Here. Take one of these. Something to think about."

I take the brochure from her and force a smile. No way would my parents pay for me to go to France, even if I wanted to go.

"I don't think so," I say.

"I'm not pushing, but scholarships are available if money's an issue. February's the deadline." She winks one of her grey-blue eyes at me and smiles.

Walking out into a blur of hunter green and navy plaid, I knock shoulders with kids every two seconds until I finally get to my locker. I stuff the brochure in my messenger bag and grab my stuff out of my locker. I need to catch up to Anna who's at the opposite end of the hallway.

Anna slams her locker shut. "Mello, oh my God, you're totally wiped out. What's the story with you?" Anna adjusts her bag on her shoulder.

"Still not sleeping."

We inch our way towards the door. "I'm getting worried about you," she says.

"I can't go Friday night. I'm totally not in the mood and I think I'm losin' it." I stick my hand out. "Hi, I'm Carmella. My sister just died, I can't sleep, I don't eat, and I've got boy phobia so I can't speak."

Anna stops and rolls her eyes. "Mello, you seriously need to get out. And you need a distraction. This Howie and Jeremy thing is perfect." Anna leans to the side and peeks down the hall. "Madison and the girls are right over there. Let's talk to them about Friday night."

Anna's got to drive me over to Donny this afternoon. "Anna, I'll go Friday, but you need to do me a favor." I take a deep breath. "I want to go talk to Donny. I'm worried about him and think I'll sleep better if I talk to him. So you give me a ride into the city, and I'll go to the game and sit with two perfect strangers even though I've suddenly come down with a boy phobia. *And* I'll lower my standards and make nice-nice with the bitches, okay?"

"Francesca's Donny? How do you know he's even around?"

"I don't. When we get outside, I'll call him."

"If seeing him will help you, fine. But I gotta be honest, don't you think he's sort of a creep?"

"He loved her. She loved him. How could I think he was a creep?"

"I dunno." Anna's eyes shift. "My parents said they talked to your dad at the wake. He said Donny's to blame for everything."

My blood boils, I want to scream at Anna. *It's not his fault. This is all my fault,* but I don't.

"Well he's not and you've never met him. Are you gonna take me or not?"

"Fine, but you're totally getting a sweet deal on this."

"What do you mean, sweet?"

"*I* have to drive *you* into the city, which is torture to me. All *you* have to do is sit with the two cutest guys on the planet (and your friends) and watch a volleyball game," Anna says.

"Your friends," I squawk at Anna.

"Okay, my friends."

"Which is torture to me."

"Mello, this will not be torture. Trust me. We've always wanted to try the double date thing, right?"

Exhausted from Anna-logic, I pull my phone out to call Donny.

***

Anna stops at the light in the middle of downtown, right in front of the Elmwood Park Post Office. Across the street is *The Country Cobbler* shoe store Mom used to take Francesca and me to when we were kids. When Francesca was old enough to drive, we would take Mom's credit card and go ourselves to one of their end of the season sales. We each were allowed one pair. I usually went for the trendy shoes, trying new styles, but Francesca stuck with shoes she was familiar with, that were reliable and comfortable. Her ultimate favorite shoes were her Converse. One year we decided to buy matching pairs.

I'll never go back into that shoe store.

Anna turns the corner and we merge onto the expressway, towards the city.

Cars pass and cut us off because Anna's only going forty-five miles an hour on the Edens Expressway, where everyone goes at least seventy.

Anna chomps down hard on her gum. "Isn't this going to be weird, without Francesca and everything?"

"Not sure. I guess I'll find out."

Anna might be my best friend but she'll never get what I'm going through. I lost my big sister, the one person who knew all my secrets and who loved me despite my faults. When she died, a big piece of me died too.

Anna weaves in and out of traffic. "Why a bar, anyhow? We're not even supposed to be in a bar. Why couldn't we meet him at the apartment?"

I whip my head over and stare at her.

She winces. "Oh yeah. That was totally stupid. I'm sorry." She blows a giant bubble and sucks it in.

Biting my lip, a semi truck passes us. I squeeze my hands together. What if Anna's right? I've never spent more than ten minutes alone with Donny. What if we sit in total awkward silence, staring at each other? What if he brings up the fight he had with Dad when we packed up Francesca's stuff? I wiggle my toes around the inside of my Catholic school mandatory penny loafers.

Anna accidentally cuts a yellow VW Beetle off, scaring the shit out of me, trying to change lanes. She swerves back into our lane.

I let out a shriek and slap my chest with my left hand.

"I tell you, people drive like maniacs on this expressway."

"Shit, Anna. What the hell? You sure you passed your driving test? Maybe I should drive home."

"Or maybe you should have had borrowed a car from your parents."

I grab onto the armrest on the door, surprised at how Anna's killer aggressiveness in sports doesn't translate very well to her driving abilities.

"You know my parents banned me from driving. And I don't want to push the issue. They fight about everything lately."

Anna squeezes the wheel. "So, you sure we're not going to get arrested? We're not old enough to be in a bar."

I take a deep breath. "They serve burgers after five. We can't get arrested for eating."

***

We pull down the side street off of North Avenue in Old Town. The sky is all grey like rain or snow is on the way. My hands are shaky. Anna spends the next twenty minutes parallel parking while I rehearse in my head what I plan on saying to Donny. We walk up the street to Grizzly's, the corner bar where he works. A fake bear stands in front of the door with its arms outstretched, like it's going to attack. The bar owners change the bandana according to seasons and holidays. An orange, red and yellow bandana is tied around its neck today.

As I pull the wooden door open, I smell cigarettes, rotten wood and beer. Anna and I walk in, her feet practically on top of my heels. The woman bartender with long shiny black hair parted in the middle and tied in a pony glances up at us as she wipes her hands with a towel. Guys and girls sit along the bar, which extends to the other end of the room where two pool tables stand unused. Empty booths line the wall opposite the bar. I don't see Donny anywhere. We're totally out of place, like we're crashing a party.

Anna and I take a few more steps, our feet sticking to the floor. Guys on wooden stools glance over at us. The lights are dim, so I blink fast to try and focus my eyes.

Finally, a guy about Francesca's age turns around. "You're lookin' for Donny, right?"

I nod.

He points to the back of the bar and at the same time I spot Donny walking towards us. He's wearing a black baseball cap, black leather jacket and a black T-shirt. Even in this light, he looks pasty and his eyes are bloodshot and glassy. I should smile at him, but I'm shocked. He looks worse than he did when I saw him last.

He grabs me and gives me a hug. The smell of leather, cigarettes and whiskey practically knocks me over. He reeks like he's soaked with sweat and his hair smells sour. I'm guessing he hasn't showered in days. I gag a little bit.

Donny releases me from his grip and turns to Anna. "Hey, you must be Anna, the driver."

She shakes Donny's hand, then smiles and shifts her feet. She's freaked out big time. "What can I get you girls to drink?" he asks.

I clear my throat. Everyone is staring at us. I swear I hear a whisper about girls in a uniform looking hot. I want to run.

"Oh, nothing. I'm okay. We can't stay long. I have a ton of homework to catch up on."

Donny pulls out a roll of money from his front pocket. "C'mon. I had a good week and you two obviously came right from school. You must be thirsty. You need an after school pick me up? How 'bout a Coke, root beer, beer? Shot of Crown Royal? Shit. Whatever you want. It's on me."

Anna sticks her hands into the pockets of her black wool hooded coat, chewing her gum.

I want to leave right now but we're stuck. "Okay, I guess a Diet Coke then," I say. Why did I think seeing Donny would make me feel better?

"Me too, thanks," Anna says.

She pokes me. "There's two guys at the bar staring. They're like my dad's age. It's totally creeping me out."

I turn my head.

"No, don't look at them." Anna grabs my elbow, squinting her eyes at me.

Donny comes back holding a bottle of Budweiser. "Let's go over here." He points with his pinky to a booth next to the pool tables in the back and starts walking.

"Haley's got the rest of the drinks."

Anna and I follow Donny. He slides in on one side of the wooden booth. We slide in on the other. Donny asks me how my parents are and we make small talk about the weather and school for a few minutes.

The bartender comes over with a tray of drinks. She sets down two pints of Diet Coke with red straws in front of Anna and me, and two shots of Crown Royal whiskey in front Donny.

"Thanks, darlin'." Donny winks at her.

She smiles and winks back, then prances away.

I fidget in my seat. I'm kind of ticked off Donny's flirting with another girl, like he's cheating on Francesca.

"So how are you?" Donny asks.

"Okay," I lie.

"You don't look okay."

"I can't sleep. I don't want to eat much."

Donny holds up his shot glass, then drinks down the whiskey. "Couple of these and a downer and sleep's not a problem. Here, you want a couple?" Donny reaches into his jacket.

"No."

"Why not?"

I want to slap Donny across the face. How could he think about drinking and doing drugs after holding Francesca's dead body in his arms on the bathroom floor?

Anna nudges me with her elbow.

I didn't imagine a meeting with Donny going like this. For some reason, I figured after what happened to Francesca, Donny would be terrified to drink or do drugs. I thought he'd be all straight, maybe sober up in honor of her if he didn't want to do it for himself. I want to scream at him, but I can't. I can't even look at him.

"Donny, we should go. Anna's terrified of driving on the expressway."

"But you haven't even had a sip of the drinks I bought you yet. Chill out."

I've got to get out of here, away from Donny. My plan is to act all torn up inside, too hurt to talk. We'll make a quick exit.

Donny holds up his beer bottle and points to me. "Remember, Carm, when Fran introduced me to the family when we first started dating? They all loved me."

"Yeah."

"Has Anna heard the story of how Frannie and I met?"

"No," Anna does a fake smile. The kind she does when she's nervous. "I don't know anything about you and Francesca."

"Pure love at first sight. We were both at a party in Evanston," he says. "Francesca walked in on her boyfriend making out with her best friend. We literally ran into each other as she was storming out of the party. She was bawling her eyes out. We started talking and never left the front stoop. I was working at the Board of Trade at the time, working my freakin' ass off and had no idea why.

"So, you don't trade anymore?" she asks.

"Nah. Gave it up. I work here now." Donny smiles at Anna then takes another drink of his beer.

"You're kidding, why?"

He winks at Anna and leans over the table. "Listen, sweetheart, I decided to stop chasing my tail. I should have given up when my dad told me to give up, way back when I didn't make it into Princeton or Harvard, where all his friends' kids went. Northwestern was a cop out to him. And being a trader? Who cares I had tons of money and was living on the North Shore of Chicago with my BMW? Eventually, I stopped trying to prove something to the world."

"So you think success means trying to prove something?" she asks.

I turn to Anna. "Shit, you Dr. Phil or something?" A hammer hits me in the head. Donny's had a lot to drink. He's spilling his guts. I have to get us out of here before he says something stupid and makes Francesca look bad. Anna doesn't know anything about Donny and I want to keep it that way.

"We should go." I grab Anna's arm with my left hand, my right hand on the table.

Donny leans forward and puts his hand on top of mine. "C'mon, you just got here."

Anna starts sliding out of the booth. "I think Mello's right, we're going to hit traffic."

"Wait, sis. You sounded shitty on the phone and you look like shit. Besides, talking about these things is what those mother f'ing shrinks say we should do, right?"

The pain in Donny's eyes stops me. He's the only one who knew Francesca like I did. I owe it to her to sit and listen to her boyfriend, but I have to get rid of Anna.

"Okay, maybe just a few minutes." I turn to Anna. "You wanna hit the ladies' room before we get back on the road?"

Anna takes a sip of her Diet Coke, her eyes shift back and forth, and then she gets my hint. "Good idea." She slides out of the booth.

He smiles and takes off his hat, revealing his dishwater blonde hair and crystal blue eyes. He drinks down his second shot. I stare at the empty glass for a second, remembering the first time I was alone with Donny when Francesca left to go down to the laundry room. He told me the story of how his dad raised him and his sister after their mother died in a car wreck. He had a few too many Crown Royals, and confessed to me how he thought his mother's death was his fault. If he had taken the bus to school like he was supposed to, the car that ran the stop sign wouldn't have hit her. She would have been at work.

Donny wipes his mouth with the side of his hand and stares into my eyes. "So."

I watch the ice cubes float at the top of my glass and twirl my hair. I wonder if Donny's dreaming about her like I am.

"You dream about Francesca?" I take a sip of my Diet Coke.

"I don't remember dreams. Do you?"

"Yeah, I dream about her every night. They seem so real, like she's in the room with me, I wonder if I'm losing my mind."

"She's probably visiting you. I've heard of it happening to lots of people." Donny smiles.

"Really? So I'm not going nutty?"

"Nah." He reaches across the table and puts his hand on mine again. I pull my hand back and put it in my lap. I squeeze my fingers while I stare at the bathroom, the door closing behind Anna.

Donny takes a swig of his beer. "Too bad none of us said goodbye. That's the problem. People always think there's a tomorrow. You know, the people I really feel sorry for are your parents."

I sniff. "No kidding. They're really messed up, I'm not sure if they'll ever get over this."

"That's not what I mean."

"What do you mean?"

"I mean, I'm sure they feel like shit about how they treated Francesca, and now they can't say they're sorry."

"What are you talking about? My parents were never mean to Francesca."

Donny shakes his head, peering into my eyes. "She sure did a good job of hiding it from you."

"Hiding what?"

"Carmella. Didn't you ever see that Francesca sheltered you from reality?"

"What reality? I don't know what you're talking about."

"Francesca always felt like she was less of a daughter to them, less loved. She felt like she was always a disappointment to your parents. She felt like she was less of a human being, period."

"What? That's crazy. What are you talking about? My parents loved Francesca. They never said she was less than anything. I'm the one who should feel that way. They never paid any attention to me, they were always so worried about her."

Donny cuts me off. "They never came out and said it, but it was there. You were always the one they bragged about, you were the one they would talk up in front of the family. Didn't you ever notice? It was always, Carmella's such a great student, we're so proud of her. You're totally their favorite. It ate her up inside."

"You're crazy, she told me everything and she never said anything about this."

"You're right. She never told you because she didn't want you to feel bad. I'm only telling you this because I loved Francesca and I know how shitty she felt every day. You should know what she did for you, standing around and listening to your parents brag about how great you are, her whole life."

"You're drunk." I start to slide out of the booth.

Donny reaches over and grabs my forearm. "Her and I, we had the same kind of screwed up parents. You shouldn't deny what she did for you."

My eyes fixate on Donny's face. I can't seem to move. I'm terrorized with the idea of Francesca feeling so hurt and never telling me. How did I not see this? Donny must be lying. He must be saying this to blame me when, in fact, it's his fault that Francesca's dead. Why else would he say this to me?

"You're lying. You pressured her to take those pills, didn't you? That's why you're making all this up. You feel guilty."

Donny leans forward, his leather coat cracks, he lowers his voice. "I don't feel guilty about Francesca. But I think you might."

"No I don't. I wasn't with her. I didn't know she was in trouble. I thought she was just partying and having fun—with you." I hate myself for not seeing the truth, for not wanting to believe Francesca had a problem.

"Sure Frannie and I were having a good time. But you know in your heart, Carmella, that you're the only person Francesca would listen to, but you didn't *do* anything. So face facts. You're gonna feel like shit the rest of your life. And you know what else? I wonder if Mommy and Daddy are gonna think differently of their favorite little girl when they find out you knew about Francesca's drinking and doing drugs for the past year, but didn't tell them. I'd think about telling them the truth before they hear it from someone else's lips."

The earth shifts on its axis. I slide out of the booth. "You are such as asshole."

Donny slides out of the booth and grabs my forearm.

I try to break free of his grip but he pinches my arm. He stands in front of me. I pull my arm away and bolt towards the restroom.

Donny yells at me. "Hating me for telling you the truth won't change anything. What's done is done. Now you have to figure out how to live with yourself."

I spin my head around. "You should know," I blurt out. I hold back the rest of what I want to say to Donny but don't have the guts. Inside my head, I think, *yeah, you should know, Mr. I'm going to slowly kill myself because I think I killed my mother.*

"Whatever. You got my number and I'm the only person who knows the truth. Mark my words, you'll be calling me."

"Yeah? I'll call you when hell freezes over." I yank the door open. Anna's standing in the bathroom texting. "We're going," I yell.

The two of us race out of the bar, practically running to the car.

Anna says, gasping for breath, "Mello. Shit. What happened?"

I stick my arm out. "Nothing. Just give me the keys. We gotta get outta here."

***

As we drive down North Avenue, my hands squeeze the steering wheel tight, and my eyes are glued to the road.

Anna turns to me. "Mello. Are you gonna tell me what Donny said? You're scaring me."

I merge onto the expressway, the white lines blurred. "I can't. I have to focus. Seeing him was a mistake."

"Obviously," she says.

I follow the red taillights in front of me.

"That bar was pretty scary. I'm surprised how Donny looks. I didn't picture him so strung out. You didn't describe him as so …"

I cut Anna off. "I don't want to talk about him. I don't want to talk, okay?"

After a few minutes, Anna turns on her country music. "So you had a fight with him?"

"Yeah."

"My parents said when you lose people, all sorts of buried feelings come to the surface."

I glance over at Anna and back to the road. "What the hell are you talking about? Have you ever lost anything bigger than your magenta pink Crayola crayon? Oh my God."

"I'm just repeating what my parents said to me. We talked about this so I could help you."

"Oh brother. Poor Carmella and her pathetic dead sister and their family, it will be so hard for them to get through all their *buried* feelings."

"Mello. You're totally being a bitch. I'm trying to help. Why are you being so mean?"

"Because. You and your family know nothing about mine. For your information, we don't have anything buried because we don't have any secrets. We talk. We talk, okay?"

Anna glares at me. "Whatever happened between you and Donny, you don't have to take it out on me. I'm not the enemy."

My hands ache from holding onto the steering wheel so tight.

After ten minutes of silence, I wish I didn't yell at Anna but it is so hard for me to be with her now. In four weeks, I've been thrown into a world where I am clueless on how to survive. Nothing in my life will be the same and I could lose everyone if I tell the truth about Francesca taking drugs, and me not telling anyone. Especially Anna. No way could she understand any of this.

I glance over at her. "I'm sorry. That talk with Donny sucked. I thought he was someone I could talk to but now I see I can't. He makes me feel like ..."

Anna looks at me. "Like what?"

I can't tell Anna Donny made me realize I have to keep what I knew about Francesca doing drugs a secret for the rest of my life. I'm scared to think about him telling my parents. I can't even go there right now. I can't talk about this with anyone, especially Anna. "It isn't important. He was drunk."

Anna fishes into her purse for a new piece of gum. "Gum?"

"Sure." I take the piece of gum from Anna and focus on the road, hoping the ride will go quick.

Anna changes the subject and fills me in on all the gossip going around the girls' volleyball team. I barely listen. And then about ten minutes away from my house, Anna mentions Friday night in a very transparent attempt at cheering me up.

Chapter 4

Reasons why I should keep what I knew about Francesca a secret until I die

1. Telling the truth won't bring Francesca back.
2. Anna will pretend not to hate me but then slowly sneak away, like I won't notice she's gone.
3. My mother won't hate me but will never look at me the same.
4. My father will hate me forever.

Reasons why I should keep on living

1. I made a promise to Anna to go to that stupid game on Friday night.
2. If I kill myself, I'll go to hell.
3. Mom and Dad don't deserve to lose two daughters because of my one screw up.

Sitting in my closet with the door open, I stare out at the black sky, thinking about what Donny said at the bar. An inferno erupts in my stomach. Was he telling me the truth? My whole body hurts at the thought of Francesca thinking she wasn't good enough. She was the best to me. She wasn't afraid of breaking the rules to get what she wanted and she could be so funny when the mood struck her. She wasn't someone who would get a whole room laughing, but when she was with only one or two friends, she'd have them all cracking up big time. She and I had a blast no matter what we did, even doing the dreaded spring window washing chore was fun. And we never got sick of being around each other. The only time we fought was over clothes. I'd give anything to take back all those fights about the summer Fourth of July tank top I stole from her or the favorite black sweater she borrowed from me and stretched out because she didn't like to wear things tight.

The kitchen door squeaks open downstairs. I get up and peek out my bedroom window, which faces the back yard and the garage. Mom's home. Her keys jingle and the closet door in the foyer slides open. "Carmella? You upstairs?"

I'm afraid to answer. I'm afraid she's going to tell me Donny talked to her. I pissed him off, he had a few more shots of whiskey, then he called my parents and told them the truth.

I stand at the top of the steps, and squeeze my pencil. "Yeah?"

"Come down here."

"Why?"

"I want to talk to you, that's why."

"Okay, what?" My heart pounds faster.

My mother puts her hand on her hip. "Are you going to just stand there?"

I walk down the steps.

My mother turns and walks into the kitchen. She opens the fridge and takes out a bottle of cold red wine and pours a glass. She leans on the counter and folds her arms up in front of her.

"Carmella...I *need* you to go to confession."

"Is that it? You want me to go talk to a priest?"

"Yes, Father Carlucci."

"Why?"

"Because I'm worried about you, so I arranged a meeting."

"You've never worried about me before."

"Well, I never needed to worry about you until now. I set up a three-thirty confession."

"I'm not going."

"Yes you are. And please stop arguing with me. You used to be so agreeable."

I want to say *I used to be so agreeable because I was invisible to you.* But I don't say that to her. I don't want to make her upset. "I don't need any help. And especially from a priest."

My mother throws her arms up in the air. "Carmella."

"Can I go back upstairs now?"

"Not until you agree to go talk to Father Carlucci. I think a blessing from him will clear your conscience."

"You think I need to clear my conscience?"

"Doesn't everybody?"

"I told you, I don't need any help. And I am not going to go confess my deepest, darkest secrets to a priest who totally blanked out on Francesca's name at her funeral. You can't make me go talk to that asshole."

"Carmella, don't you dare use that language when talking about a priest." My mother does the sign of the cross. "It wasn't his fault that Francesca stopped going to church. Of course he wouldn't remember her name."

"I don't care what kind of excuses you make for him, I'm not going."

My mother rubs the side of her face. "What about another priest, like Father Charlie? Remember he taught your forth grade scripture class for a while and you liked him a lot? We can call him."

"No way. I have to work."

Mom scratches her head and sweeps her hair behind her ear. "If you go to confession with Father Charlie tomorrow, I'll let you take the car to school. But only tomorrow." She rests her hand on her hip.

"When are you going to let me drive every day like I used to?"

"I don't know. I'm not comfortable thinking about you behind the wheel of a car."

My mother seems so stressed. "If I go, will you stop worrying like a crazy person and let me drive again?"

"I went today and I think it really helped. Please go, for me."

My mother looks pale and wiped out. Maybe if I do this, she'll feel better. Besides, I remember Father Charlie. He wasn't like a regular priest. He talked about life, and he was pretty cool. It's only an hour out of my life.

"Do you think Father Charlie's available?"

"Not sure. But everyone at church is very eager to help us. I'll call right now. I'm sure he'll make time for you."

"This is going to screw up Mrs. Sparacini's schedule."

My mother lets out a deep breath and shakes her head. "You're only going to be an hour late. I'm sure under the circumstances, she'll understand."

I turn to go back up into my room when the kitchen door flies open and my father walks in. The three of us exchange looks. I don't know what to say. Usually this would be a time when my parents would ask me about Francesca. She'd avoid their calls, but still talk to me, so I became the go-between. But the last month before she died she didn't even talk to me.

My dad hangs his keys up, and then walks into his office off the kitchen and sets his bag down. He walks past us into the foyer to hang up his coat without saying or looking at either of us.

I wait for him to acknowledge my mother or me, but he doesn't. The three of us are trying to be normal but everything is off, everything is wrong. Francesca's gone and now we have no reason to talk.

He takes a bottle of beer out of the fridge. There's a plate of leftovers on the counter with a cover for him, ready to go into the microwave. As my father puts his dinner in and pushes three buttons, I imagine the expression on his face when I tell him I knew Francesca was doing drugs. I wonder if he'd hate me.

My father turns around. "You should be in bed. You look tired."

My mother takes a drink. "Carmella and I were talking and she's agreed to go to confession tomorrow."

"Since when?" my father asks.

"Since today. Carmella's obviously having trouble dealing with all this, so I arranged for her to go to confession."

"Why didn't we discuss this first? You did this behind my back?"

"No, I just want Carmella to go talk to someone. I figured you'd agree."

"That's not the point. I need to know what's going on in my house." My dad's voice cracks.

"What's the big deal?"

"I need to know when you're sending my daughter to talk to someone." My dad turns to me. "Don't bring up the drugs. It was an accident and we don't need to keep harping on it."

My dad turns towards the kitchen window, his back is to us.

"Joe, Francesca died of an overdose. Carmella might need help dealing with her feelings."

He turns around to face us. "I can't stand it when you say 'overdose' like that. It was an accident. Why can't you accept it was an accident?"

"Why can't you accept she might have had a problem?"

"My daughter did not have any problems. I think you want to blame it on an addiction because *you* don't want to face the fact that if you would have listened to me and not supported her decision to move in with Donny, she would still be alive right now. But you had to go against me, didn't you?"

"Joe, this has nothing to do with you. I was desperate for Francesca to be happy for once. First we thought middle school adjustment was the problem, then we thought high school social pressures were getting to her, then we thought maybe college would be the answer, but it wasn't. I was trying."

"Well, you made a mistake."

I can't listen to my parents argue about Francesca anymore. They've been at it nonstop since the funeral. "I saw Donny today."

Both my parents' faces fall.

"You what?" My father's neck bulges.

"I talked to Donny today."

"Why the hell is he calling you?" he asks.

"He didn't call me, I called him."

"You called him? For what?" My mother sits down.

I wonder if I should tell them the truth about knowing Francesca was doing drugs, or take a chance that Donny won't tell them.

"I wanted to talk to him so I went to the bar."

My father steps closer to me. "What? How?"

"Anna drove me."

"He hunted you down for money, didn't he?" Dad says pacing the floor.

"No, it wasn't like that. I was curious. I dream about Francesca every night and I wondered if he did too."

Dad shakes his head. "You what?"

My mother puts her head in her hands. "You and Anna drove all the way into the city? You could have gotten in an accident." My mother lifts her head up. "You must be covering for Donny. How much money did you give him?"

"I didn't give him any money. I told you, I wanted to know if he was having dreams."

My mother gets up and pulls a tissue out of the yellow box on the counter. "Good thing you're seeing Father Charlie."

"I still think you're lying," my father says.

"He loved Francesca and misses her like I do."

"I would have expected this type of thing from Francesca, she was always doing things behind our back, but not from you," Dad says.

His tone makes me feel two inches tall, like I've committed a crime. "Why don't you believe me?" I ask.

"Never speak to Donny again, understood? You have no business talking to him. You have no reason to keep in contact with him. I've still got work to do." My father turns around and walks into his office, shutting the door behind him.

My mother stares out the window over the sink. "Carmella, please don't ever drive into the city without telling us. And your father's right. You don't need to be in contact with Donny. You need to talk to people who can help you."

I stare at my mother's back. She turns around, walks up to me and wraps her arms around me. I want to feel her hug, but I can't.

"Are you okay?" My mother cradles my face in her hands, staring into my eyes.

She gives me a kiss on the cheek. "I think you're having those dreams because you're so overtired. Go get some rest. I'm going to bed too."

"I need a glass of water."

My mother walks out of the kitchen. I open the cabinet next to the sink and grab a tall glass from the second shelf. I pour water into my glass and hear a strange noise coming from my dad's office. I walk closer to the door. It's my dad. He's crying. His agony seeps through the bottom of the door and stabs me right in my heart.

***

After brushing my teeth and washing my face, I crawl into bed. Before I turn the light out, my mother taps on my door. "Yeah?" I sit up.

She walks in and sits down on the edge of the bed. "I called the rectory. Father Charlie's available after school tomorrow. I put a donation envelope in your bag. Make sure you hand it to Mrs. Malloy who works there when you go. And here's half a sleeping pill. Dr. Marchetti said you could take it."

My mother's face is all scrunched up and worried. She kisses the top of my head and walks out. The door closes behind her. I turn out the light and lie down, closing my eyes, the image of Francesca's face plastered against my eyelids. I open my eyes and stare at the light from the moon above my bed and the blackness all around it.

Then I hear my parents' voices. The volume gets louder. I squeeze my eyes together and cover my ears with my pillow to try and drown out the shouting but I can still hear them. The sound of shattering glass scares me. I turn on the light, grab my pillow and wrap my arms around it like a teddy bear.

The sliding door of the foyer closet opens, then another door slams. I flinch. I turn out my light, crawl out of bed and inch my way over to the window. My father walks into the garage and in a minute, I see the garage door open and him drive away. I wonder where he's going. I wonder what my mother's doing.

Slowly, I pull the door of my bedroom open and tiptoe down the steps. I freeze. My mother's on her hands and knees, bawling her eyes out, picking up pieces of her broken glass, red wine streaming down the kitchen wall.

I turn around and race back up the steps and into my bedroom and close the door. I'm afraid to face her. What would I say? Francesca's gone and now my parents hate each other and this is all my fault.

I inch my way back to my bed and swallow the sleeping pill my mother left on my nightstand. I squeeze my eyes shut and recite the *Our Father* prayer over and over.

I smell cigarette smoke.

I sit straight up and watch a shadow move across Francesca's side of the room.

"Are you here?" I whisper into the air.

The shadow stops at Francesca's bed.

The wind howls, but the trees outside my window are still. The wind sound dies down. My hands shake. I wrap my arms around my body. I try to whisper Francesca's name, but I can't. I hug my knees to my chest and breathe in the smell of cigarette smoke, terrified Francesca might be in my room, and thrilled that she's here at the same time.

I whisper, "I didn't mean to do the wrong thing."

The shadow moves toward the window, whispering and a quiet howl fill my room.

I want to run after the shadow but I'm too afraid. So I sit on my bed and let the tears trickle down my face as I watch the shadow shrink into the darkness of the night.

Chapter 5

List of how I can get my father and mother to love me again

1. Agree with them.
2. Let them rule my life.
3. Bring back Francesca.
4. Pray.

Hundred-two-year-old Mrs. Malloy smiles and takes the donation envelope from me. I've never been inside the rectory. She closes the door. Mothballs and hospital disinfectant fills the air, the scent of living in holiness, I guess. There are medieval looking light fixtures hanging down from the way higher than normal ceiling. I wonder if the high ceiling makes you closer to God.

Mrs. Malloy smiles as she directs me with her hand into a large living room. She tells me I can sit anywhere and that Father Charlie will be in at three thirty sharp. There are two couches on either side of a coffee table and one chair off to the side. I decide to sit on the end of the couch, setting my messenger bag down next to me on the floor. I look up at the ceiling. There's got to be a connection to the heavens or something in here. The grandfather clock is going to ring once in about two minutes. I wonder if Father Charlie is going to tell me I'm going to hell.

Bong. Father Charlie walks in as the grandfather clock echoes three thirty. He closes the solid oak door and turns to me with a smile.

He extends his hand out. "Miss D'Agostino. Good to see you. My, you've grown."

I start to stand up.

"No, not necessary, please." Father Charlie shakes my hand.

I sit back down on the couch. He's wearing the regular black priest shirt with the white collar, but instead of the usual black pants he's wearing Levi's and a black belt. His hands are covered in age spots, and feel like sandpaper. He's clutching a Bible in his left hand. He's wearing wire-rimmed glasses, his light brown eyes smiling even when he's not.

I straighten my uniform skirt. I'm sure Father Charlie must have some kind of superhuman-priest-X-ray to-your-soul vision. The brown leather chair crunches as he sits.

"Let's begin," he says.

"Okay." I clear the fur ball from my throat. I haven't been this nervous since I was sent to the principal's office in middle school.

"Confession?" He smiles.

"Um, should I say the usual thing?" Which would be good if I could remember the usual thing. My brain seems to have left my body.

"Whatever you're comfortable with."

"Okay. Bless me, Father, for I have sinned. It's been, um, one month? Since my last confession." I squeeze my hands together.

I can't look him in the eyes, so I glance past him, over his right shoulder, out the paned window at the willow tree that sits in the middle of the rectory's front lawn. The last time I went to confession was before any of this happened. I'm sure I didn't confess that I was lying because I didn't think I was. How screwed up is that? I think I confessed my usual guilt about going to church every Sunday only because I had to, not because I wanted to, and not praying every day.

Father Charlie must be waiting for me to confess something.

"Go on," he says.

Could you give me a blessing so I don't go to hell for lying? That's what I want to say, but I'm scared there's a secret hole underneath the couch and Father Charlie will press a button and I'll go flying down, right into the gates of hell. So I say, "I lied. And I can't seem to do anything right these days."

"To whom did you tell a lie?" Father Charlie tilts his head.

"To everyone. To my mother, my father."

"Everyone. Are you sure you lied to everyone? Is there anyone in your life that you didn't lie to?"

"My sister. I never lied to her."

Father Charlie's eyes lower with the tone of his voice. "I'm sorry about your sister. So was this lie something having to do with her?"

"Yes."

"You'd like forgiveness from the Lord for your actions?"

"Yes."

"Let us pray."

I'm shocked. Is Father Charlie going to let this go without some kind of ritualistic punishment? I recite the Our Father, wondering what's going to happen next. Father Charlie closes his eyes and as I say the prayer with him, I wonder why he isn't asking me more questions, like what the lies were, or why I told them. I wonder if he's tricking me. Father Charlie's eyes are shut tight, his hands suspended in the air, like he's summonsing God for me. I stare at the floor, my eyelids lowered enough so it seems like they're closed. We chant the Our Father again. I go along with it, the whole time hoping that my mother feels better about this because as he keeps praying, I keep thinking God's going to send a bolt of lightning down from heaven and slice me in two. We say the Hail Mary ten times.

Father Charlie clears his throat, stands up, and while his hand is suspended in the air over my head, he recites a few Psalms from his book.

"Repeat 'Amen' with me," he says.

"Amen." I stare at his black shoes.

He closes the prayer book and sits back down in his overstuffed brown leather chair.

"Carmella. I understand you are here because your mother thought you should speak with someone, yes?"

I swallow. "Yes."

"This must be an extremely difficult time for all of you. Do you know why your mother sent you here to talk to me?"

"She's worried about me."

"How so?" Father Charlie adjusts his glasses.

I glance over at the clock. I want to run. "I'm not eating much and I'm waking up with dreams every night."

"Are any of those dreams about your sister?"

I turn my head away and stare at Jesus hanging on the cross. I turn my head back and look at Father Charlie. "Sometimes."

"You miss her."

I nod.

"Do those dreams of Francesca scare you?"

"I don't know if they scare me, but what scares me is how real they feel." I hope Father Charlie doesn't think I'm crazy.

"Dear Carmella, God works in mysterious ways and it is very common for our loved ones to come back and visit us. Never be afraid of things you cannot explain." Father Charlie adjusts his gold wire-rimmed glasses. "Carmella, death is one of life's greatest mysteries. The pain of losing someone we love is the biggest cross we have to bear, and for someone like you, so young, it is more than you should have to handle. But know that God is with her, and God is with you. Hold onto your faith in yourself and keep praying for strength. I promise, God will see you through this."

Father Charlie smiles at me and for a second, the ache of never seeing Francesca again goes away. Then I remember he didn't ask me more about the lying. Is he going to bring in reinforcements before he asks me to go into more detail?

Father Charlie walks over to me, puts his hand out over my head, closes his eyes and mumbles, "I ask our Lord to grant you peace." Father Charlie moves his hand to my shoulder and opens his eyes.

"Remember, Carmella. God never gives us more than we can handle. Go in peace."

Did he say go? Wow. Okay, I guess I lucked out. I pick up my messenger bag and throw it over my shoulder as I follow Father Charlie into the foyer.

***

It's hard to believe it's Friday. I haven't seen or spoken to Dad since the other night when I heard him crying in his office and saw him storm out of the house after the huge fight. I still think about my mom wiping the wine off the wall. Dad's been conveniently working later than usual. Midwest Restaurant Supply is their biggest client ever, and the sprinkler system broke in their offices and warehouse. That means Dad has to work until eleven at night supervising the disaster recovery and restoration that's going around the clock. "Nature of the business," he says. I wonder how he'll avoid being home when he's done helping them recover from their disaster.

Standing here watching for Hannah's car, I can't remember why the hell I'm doing this. Oh yeah. I made a promise to Anna. I'd give anything to be able to crawl into my bed and hide from the world.

Hannah pulls up in her dad's ancient silver four-door Camry and beeps a few times. Madison's in the front seat with her, so I slip into the back with Izzy, who's swirling on lip gloss.

"Hi." I click my seatbelt and fish out some lip stuff too.

Anna and I decided not to tell the rest of the girls about meeting Jeremy and Howie at the game, mostly because Madison's got this wicked competitive streak in her and she'd come into the situation and be sure to steal one of them away. We didn't want to give her three days to plan her boy-stealing strategy. Plus she's on my permanent shit list for being such a bitch all the time.

Madison switches her iPod to a Kanye West song, snapping her fingers to the music, her long light brown hair moving to the beat. Izzy clears her throat and runs her fingers through her dark, almost black straight shoulder-length bob she's had since we all met. Izzy, Hannah and Madison all came from St. Luke's over in River Forest. Anna and I came from St. Celestine grade school in Elmwood Park. Anna met the girls when they all made the basketball team freshman year and I tag along because they're Anna's friends. Anna also plays volleyball but these girls don't; they run cross-country in the fall. Still, I can't relate to any of them, except for Izzy sometimes. They're rich, I'm not. They're jocks, I'm not. I'm in the Art Club and the Choir, and they for sure—are not.

Madison swings around in her seat and gives me an up and down. "Black boots and a black skirt with leggings again? And what's with the bag? Bring some bakery treats to share?"

I flash a sarcastic smile at her. "Nooo." I pull out a blue pom-pom from a Party Store bag. "Some of us think past our outfits. I got some of these to wave in the air to cheer Anna and her team on."

Izzy grabs a pom-pom out of my hand. "Great idea, Mello."

Hannah gives a quick glance towards Madison. "Bet you wish we were as thoughtful as Mello." She smirks.

Madison changes the music on the iPod to Lady Gaga. "Not really. I'm not the nurturing type. Probably why Mr. Kasper gives Mello all the Mom roles in theatre class and I get all the young daughter roles."

"Young slut roles you mean," I say.

Izzy's the only one who hears my remark. She covers her mouth, gives me a thumbs up and laughs.

***

Reasons why I hate sports

1. I'm so uncoordinated that at sixteen I can't play any sport without making a complete ass out of myself.
2. Sports are boring.
3. My most scarring memories of childhood involve being made fun of on the T-ball field.
4. If a game involves a ball, I get hit in the head—guaranteed.

When we get to school, Madison, Izzy and Hannah go straight to the bleachers. I push through the hyped-up crowd and walk into the girls' locker room searching for Anna. Finally, I spot her.

"Mello, you made it. Did you see them yet?" Anna pulls her hair through her red hair tie, dressed in her volleyball uniform. She bounces on her toes and shakes her hands out.

"No, I didn't." I open and close my hands, trying to calm my nerves. "Where are we supposed to meet?"

Anna takes a deep breath in, then out. "Right outside the gym."

Olivia, one of Anna's teammates, whizzes by us. "Let's go, Fitz!"

Anna puts her hands on top of my shoulders, "Mello, thanks for coming. And chill out about the guys. It's no big deal. You'll be fine."

I nod. I really do not want to do this.

Olivia grabs Anna's arm, "Fitz! Now!"

"I gotta go, Mello. " Anna runs backwards towards the door. "Find Jeremy and Howie. I'll catch up with you after the game. I'm totally psyched. This is gonna be awesome."

"Good luck. We'll be out there cheering for you," I shout to the closed door. *Oh my God, why did I agree to this?*

***

Pacing outside the doors of the gym, I think they blew us off. I've been out here for a super long time. Everyone's inside, the game's gonna start any second. Giving up on Jeremy and Howie, I stuff my phone into my purse and head into the gym. Walking up the bleachers, I think there's a part of me that feels a little disappointed for some crazy reason. I sit down next to Izzy. Oh well. At least I don't have to sit next to Madison.

"Hey, Mello." Madison leans over as the whistle blows, the squeaking of gym shoes piercing my eardrum. "You got any gum?"

Speak of the devil. "Sure." I dig through my purse, pull out the giant pack, and pass it around to the girls. Watching them pull pieces out, I realize I'm always the one who has gum. I pop a piece in my mouth and check my phone one more time.

Everyone stands up and roars, so I throw my phone back in my purse and stand up. As I clap along with them, my eyes scan the volleyball court. I wonder if it was Anna who spiked the ball.

Izzy nudges me, waving the pom-poms. "Did you see that?"

"No. What happened?"

"Oh my God. Anna totally nailed the shot." Izzy does her finger whistle. The sound makes me jump. She waves her pom-poms again, hitting me in the face. I cringe. All of this is driving me crazy.

"Hey Mello, are you okay? You look kinda funny." Izzy's still clapping. I wave my pom-poms. The cheering stops, the crowd settles, and we sit.

"I'm fine. Kind of not in the mood for all this," I say.

"Oh, well, sure. I'm sure it's got to be hard and everything. I mean, not that I would know." Izzy quickly changes the subject. "This is gonna be a great game. I can tell they're gonna totally win big time."

I try to act like I'm having fun, secretly wishing I were sitting alone in my bedroom. Anna serves, and as I follow the ball across the net, I spot the boys. They're here. On the other side. It's Jeremy and Howie. They point to me. They wave. I wave back. Izzy watches me. They both throw their arms up in the air and gesture like they're playing charades. They point to their cell phones. Jeremy's phone died and I'm not sure if Howie lost or forgot his phone and they came in late and sat on the wrong side. Every few minutes, one of them does a goofy hand gesture, waves at me and I wave back. Izzy nudges me. She wants to know what the heck I'm doing, so I give her the whole scoop.

In the middle of the second half something happens to Anna's team. They keep missing volleys. St. Alphonsus racks up all kinds of points and finally, Anna misses a volley, bangs into her teammate and they lose the game. Right after the whistle blows, Jeremy and Howie point to the south door at the same time. Confirming what they mean, I point to the door and they nod their heads. I'm so glad the game is over, this night is over, and I can go home. I remember the Lombardo wedding tomorrow. The Lombardo cake is the biggest wedding cake Mrs. Sparacini has ever done and I know she'll need me to take care of the entire front and back for her all morning.

As we nudge our way off the bleachers, I'm sure Anna will be upset about the game. I do a little freak out when I think about talking to Jeremy and Howie. I hope Anna gets out of the locker room fast. We weave through the crowd, other kids pushing and shoving us. Izzy, Hannah and Madison follow me. They yell at me, asking me where I'm headed. Izzy tells the other girls that we're going to say hello to a couple of guys I know.

We walk through the gym doors and I spot them right away. You can totally tell they're not from Trinity. Their clothes are nicer, especially their shoes. I gulp.

"Hi." Howie walks up to me, smiling. He points to Jeremy. "Hey, you remember Jeremy, right?"

Jeremy rolls his eyes. "Funny, dude."

Madison nudges right up next to Jeremy and flashes one of her best smiles. Hannah and Izzy follow her lead like puppy dogs.

"Hi." They all chant together.

I'm ready to barf.

Jeremy and Howie say hi, both of them have their hands stuffed in their front pockets, rocking on their heels. Howie's wearing shorts again—army green.

Madison stares at me, rolling her eyes, her arms all folded in front of her, waiting for her royal introduction. She irritates the crap out of me, I'd like to skip introducing her since she's less than human, but I don't want the guys to think I'm a bitch.

I hold my hand out, "Madison, this is Jeremy and his friend—"

"Howie." He interrupts me in a fake low voice, then mimics my hand gesture and bows at Izzy and Hannah, "And you must be Jefferson and Washington."

The three of them stand there frozen.

A laugh busts out of me. That was such a dumb joke but so funny at the same time.

Jeremy points to Howie with his thumb, "I apologize. My friend Howie doesn't conform to conventional, appropriate societal agendas. And you are?"

Madison, Hannah and Izzy look at each other.

Maybe Anna's right. These boys are new and exciting. I'm still terrified of them, but Howie's stupid joke and the way he tried to talk like he was from the 1700s is funny.

"Ahem. Ahem." Howie and Jeremy do a fake clearing of their throats.

I shout over the crowd. "Oh, sorry. These are Hannah and Izzy. I mean *this is* Hannah and Izzy." People circle around us, bumping into our backs every two seconds.

"So, tough game for Anna, huh?" Howie shouts at me.

Howie's much cuter than he was the other day in the bakery.

I nod.

Madison, Izzy and Hannah all jet their hip to the side and stretch one foot out.

"So you gonna tell us how you know these guys, Carmella? Did you meet them through your sister or what? You don't have any other friends." Madison flings her head back.

Ouch. Nice stab. "No." I sneer at her. I wish I could think of a smart-ass comeback or even a coherent sentence but my inability to sleep is making it hard to think. I wonder why Anna's taking so long.

Finally my brain turns back on. "We're making a cake for Jeremy."

That sounded so stupid. Like I'm a third grader learning to put a sentence together. Great.

"What?" Madison asks.

"They came into Il Mulano. Mrs. Sparacini's makin' them a cake." I blink a few times and search the crowd for Anna. Where the heck is she?

"Listen, girls. We got this friend who's having a party. You should check it out," Jeremy says.

"Us?" My stomach totally does a back flip. Are these guys serious?

Jeremy looks behind him, then back at us. "Ah, yeah. Z-man throws the best parties, right, Howie?"

Howie smiles at me. "Always awesome. It'll be a blast. Your friend Anna will totally forget about losing the game." Howie clasps his hands together.

"We're in," Madison, Izzy and Hannah say.

Anna walks up to us, her gym bag hanging off her shoulder.

"You and your friends have just been invited to an all-expense paid trip to Z-man's party. Cocktails included," Howie says to Anna in a fake radio voice.

I laugh. All the other girls stare at him.

Anna turns to me, "Um, Mello? Olivia's drivin' me home. I don't want to be a downer on everyone's night."

"Oh, no. Wait a minute." I panic. "I … I'll go with you. I gotta get up early for work."

Howie and Jeremy both raise their arms up in the air. "Girls, girls."

"It's only eight o'clock," Jeremy says to Anna and me.

"You will not be sorry. Guaranteed laughs," Howie says.

I'm totally terrified of Howie, but at the same time, I don't want to turn this down. He's the first person to make me laugh in a long time. He's also the cutest guy, ever. I want to go. Maybe I can get Anna to change her mind.

Howie grabs her gym bag. "Here. You look like you need a hand."

"Yeah well, another time," Anna says. "Can I have my bag back? I gotta get outta here, Olivia's waiting."

Anna starts to grab her bag from Howie.

Howie pulls the bag back and laughs.

"Give me my bag, asshole." Anna grabs the bag and snatches it out of Howie's hand. Howie and Jeremy both lean backwards and put their arms up in the air like they're being arrested.

Madison puts her hand on her hip. "Good game, even though those volleys got away from you."

Anna sneers at her, spins around and pushes through the crowd. I follow her, and grab her arm when she gets past the trophy case, knowing the boys won't hear us.

"Wait, we should go. I've been sitting here dying to go home all night, but they're both really funny. Let's check it out for an hour. I can't go without you."

"Mello, you don't understand. This game was super important to me. To my team. And I blew it."

"Yeah, but what about the guys? What about you talking me into this all week? I can't spend the rest of the night with them."

"Then come with me. Olivia will give you a lift."

I stretch my neck and in between the swarms of people I spot Madison giggling, swinging her hair, her hand on Howie's shoulder. She whispers in his ear. The thought of Madison going to the party with Howie makes something inside my brain snap.

"I don't believe this. You may have lost a game, but I lost my sister. You've got three sisters, I have none and you're too upset to go to a party? And you were the one who talked me into this night telling me to get over my grief. Wow. I can see how much you were sympathizing with me." I twist the strap of my purse tighter.

Anna's eyes are like slits. "Oh my God, go to hell." She spins around and stomps away.

Anna walks down the hall, through the double doors. I can't move. My feet are glued to the floor. I should run after Anna but I'm ticked. And have to find out who Howie is, this stranger who's been able to make me laugh and for two minutes, forget about how shitty my life is. I turn around. Howie waves. Madison's almost standing on top of him. She whispers in his ear—again.

No way. I'm not letting Madison steal him. My feet go so fast I don't think they're attached to me. Francesca's face flashes through my mind and I think of one of my favorite John Lennon quotes. *When you're by yourself and there's no one else, you just tell yourself to hold on.*

Christ, if my big sister can die alone, I should be able to have the damn guts to go to a stupid party without my best friend.

Chapter 6

Francesca list of nevers

1. We'll never have a "dog paddling" contest in the swimming pool on vacation with Mom and Dad again.
2. I'll never hear Francesca swear at me after she stubs her toe on a shoe I've left in the middle of our bedroom.
3. I'll never get another "full moon warning" text from Francesca, a reminder that her Cancerian predisposition to moodiness during a full moon should be seriously considered if I'm thinking of wearing one of her favorite shirts without asking.
4. I'll never be able to whine to Francesca about the entire world pissing me off and I'll never see Francesca do her impersonation of coach Beiste from Glee complete with the cranky voice and strut to cheer me up.
5. I'll never get another Friday night lecture from Francesca, telling me how pretty I am, convincing me when I get older, girls will totally kill for my looks. I'll never hear her People magazine logic to back up the lecture: "Carmella. There are two types of beauty: cute and pretty. I'm cute. Cute is approachable. But you: you're pretty. Guys are intimidated by your classic beauty. You can't appreciate it yet. You're

too young. But wait until you get into your twenties like me. Then guys will be falling all over you. Those cute girls with those spindly legs will have nothin' on you. Trust me."

6. And I'll never jump in the car with Francesca after she's had a fight with Donny, on an Africa-hot day, turn up the air-conditioning full blast, roll the windows down all the way and belt out her favorite Green Day song, "Extraordinary Girl," at the top of our lungs.

7. But the ultimate never that hurts the most? Never having a sister who can finish almost all of my sentences.

Never.

Again.

We follow Howie's car, a cute red BMW. As soon as we exit the expressway at Gross Point Road, my stomach pings. I know we're driving to a neighborhood like the one Donny grew up in, because I remember coming here with Donny and Francesca.

I had never been to the North Shore of Chicago where Donny's from, so one afternoon the three of us piled in his car and he gave me a tour. He told me the neighborhoods near Lake Michigan look like freaking movie sets: expensive imported cars all over the place, boutiques and specialty shops with names no one can pronounce scrolled onto chic-as-shit black awnings. Massive houses plucked straight out of glossed-up magazines with perfectly landscaped yards. Yep, just like where we're at now. We're totally out of Elmwood Park.

Howie pulls down a street and as he parks his BMW, I count the shiny expensive cars lined up along both sides of the road. We hop out of Hannah's Toyota Camry as fast as we can. Where we live, everyone drives Toyotas, Chevys or Pontiacs. There aren't any of those cars on this street.

Jeremy and Howie lead us up the gated driveway to the two-story red brick mansion, the same kind of house as the one in the movie *Home Alone*, only I think this one's bigger.

"After you." Jeremy opens the door, and a loud blast of Usher hits us as soon as we get inside.

"Follow me," Howie yells. Him wearing shorts in fifty degree Chicago weather still cracks me up.

The four of us whisper how we can't believe a neighborhood only forty minutes from ours could be so different.

We walk through the foyer of the house. Every two seconds cute girls in packs of three or four stop us so they can chat Howie and Jeremy up—while doing huge hair sweeps and giggles, of course. This party scene is making my stomach churn. After what happened to Francesca, I don't think I can do this.

Izzy and Hannah are walking behind me. I turn my head. "Hey, I'm not sure I'm in the mood for this. You guys wanna go?"

Madison's whips her head around, her hair hits me in the face. "Are you kidding me? No way. Call your mother if you want to go home."

Some guy knocks into Hannah and Izzy. "Really wild stuff going on down below, ladies. You should check it out." He takes a drag from a fat cigar as he points to a glass paned door, which leads to a lower level.

They hold their hands up to their noses.

He points to the back of my head, my hair in its usual ponytail. "Nice piggytail."

"Nice nose." Madison points her finger right at him. "And it's technically a ponytail, asshole."

He smiles. "Ooh, feisty. I like it. Come see me later." He winks and walks away.

Madison smiles and totally checks out his butt.

I wonder why Madison stuck up for me. Probably some weird survival instinct or mostly because she thinks he's hot.

I take a deep breath. I guess I'm stuck here. No way can I afford cab and I'm not calling my parents. My shoulders fall. Francesca would pick me up ASAP. She was my lifeline.

Jeremy walks up to a huge keg of beer and starts pouring cups. Howie passes them over to us, and then disappears through a doorway.

"Here's to Z-man's party." Jeremy stands next to Izzy.

Howie comes back with a cup of something green, and plants himself right next to me.

There's no way I'm drinking this. I'll sneak into the kitchen and pour the beer down the sink. A guy bumps into me and foam spills all over my hand. I shake it off.

Jeremy introduces us to tons of girls and guys who keep walking by and joining in on our conversation. When they find out we're from Trinity, they kid us about wearing uniforms, teachers who are super strict and going to church during school. I think about Anna, wondering what she's doing right now.

Madison chugs her beer. "Mello, you don't drink, do you? I mean, after what happened—"

"Of course she drinks," Izzy says.

I lean towards Madison and pour most all my beer in her cup. "I don't have a problem with drinking. Some of us work on Saturdays."

Howie reaches for my cup. "Soft drink?"

"Sure," I say. "No caffeine?"

Howie smiles and walks into the kitchen. He comes back with a lemon-lime soda for me.

"Thanks," I smile.

After a few minutes, Howie makes a suggestion to go shoot some pool. He leads us downstairs to a dark wood pool table with ornately carved legs. He grabs a cue stick and passes it to me. He rubs chalk on his stick, then takes the chalk cube and twirls it on his nose, making a perfectly round blue circle on the tip.

He holds up the block of chalk in front of me. "Would you care to join me?"

I let out a huge laugh, staring at his blue nose, staring at him, wondering if he's for real. "Sure," I say.

I'm ready to jump out of my skin as he gently cradles the back of my head and rubs chalk on my nose. I laugh and try not to freak out over him invading my personal bubble. Luckily, I'm able to curb the terror that was knocking at my door a minute ago, aching to take over me, making me want to leap out of the basement like Catwoman and run for my life.

As he works on my nose, I glance into his dark eyes. They peek through his wavy hair and for a second, I forget who I am. He's generating a seismic amount of electricity rushing up and down my whole body. I hold back the urge to laugh hysterically at the seriousness in his face and how precise he's pretending to be about rubbing stupid chalk on my nose. He's being so overly dramatic— like he's making a masterpiece.

He finishes and stands back, an ultra-satisfied grin on his face.

I laugh, wiggling my nose, the chalk tickling it, the dust falling down onto the top of my lip. "The chalk feels a little funny, how do I look?"

Howie laughs. "You look marvelous, dear. Simply dashing."

"Why, thank you. I don't believe I've ever been chalked before." I laugh.

With our blue noses and cue sticks in our hands we talk about school and have a general who-the-heck-are-you question and answer session. As I learn about the realities of Howie's life, I move farther and farther away from the realities of my own. I wrestle the sadness and anger to the ground and stuff them both into a closet.

Howie laughs. "You totally aren't from around here. You have an awesome sense of humor."

"I do?" I smile. No one's ever told me that before.

Howie turns his head towards the pool table. "Hey, Jeremy, who did you call wacked?" Howie walks over to Jeremy, who's on the other side of the table.

I follow him.

"Dude," Jeremy laughs. "You're wacked. I said 'rack 'em up.'"

Howie picks up a pool stick and points it towards the girls. "Those friends of yours are soooo serious. I think they need blue noses, don't you?"

Laughing at Howie with his blue nose, I fling my head back and shrug my shoulders. "Yes, I agree." This will probably tick them off, but what the heck.

Howie walks up to Madison and plants the chalk on her nose so quick she can't stop him.

"You shithead!" Madison swats Howie's hand away.

Hannah and Izzy hold their noses and squint at Howie.

"Weirdo," Madison yells at Howie.

Howie has no idea how great it is to see Madison embarrassed. I've wanted to piss her off like this ever since the day she made me feel like a total freak show for being a virgin.

He walks up to me with a big smile. "You ... *you* think the chalk thing is funny."

I smile and nod. "Yes, I do. I think what you did there is about the funniest thing I've seen in a really long time." The girls whisper to each other as they give Howie looks as if he drew graffiti all over Madison with a marker or something.

Z-man blasts eighties disco music, holding the remote up like a microphone and announcing 'dance card flashback' hour. A blonde pops off the couch and she starts dancing with him. Howie puts my cup down on a side table, and then takes my hands and starts dancing with me. I'm shocked. He actually knows how to dance. He's got footwork and everything. He tries to twirl me, but I've never danced with a guy before so we stop for a minute so Howie can give me a mini-dance lesson on the twirl. Three songs later, I'm sweating and glad I put my black sleeveless V-neck T-shirt on underneath my sweater. I pull my sweater and my favorite silver necklaces off. They're different lengths, each one representing an earth element and I might hurt myself, we're dancing so hard. After a few more songs, the first three notes of the next song play and I know what it is right away. Green Day's "Extraordinary Girl" blasts through the basement.

Howie's voice snaps me out of my Green Day/Francesca trance.

"Yo!" Howie's waving his hands. "I bet you're into art. Mr. Z.'s got an awesome collection. Interested?"

"Oh, sorry. What?" I wonder if my face is white.

"Art. Let's go check out Mr. Z-man's art collection." Howie takes my hand. I grab my sweater and my necklaces.

Heading towards the steps, the crowd is thick around Z-man and his friends, acting like they're a rap band, so we push ourselves through. We finally get up the steps. He leads me into a huge kitchen that has a million white paneled cabinets all around. This kitchen is about as big as our living and dining rooms combined. Liquor bottles, chips, liters of pop and empty cups sit perched on top of a black shimmery marble countertop. The music is blasting and Howie gives my hand a squeeze as we make our way through, flashing me a quick smile. The tingle from his hand moves all the way into my toes. I pull my hand away, my guy phobia kicking back in, due to the seismic earthquake inside my brain after hearing Francesca's favorite song blasted downstairs. Howie grabs my hand back with another smile, obviously thinking the crowd separated us. As we inch through, I get knocked, my shoulder accidentally pushing into his armpit and we exchange another smile. I get a whiff of his scent: pine trees and ginger. Being this close to him is like heaven and hell at the same time.

Someone calls out Howie's name and one of the guys in the crowd shoves another cup into my hand, then into Howie's. Howie shrugs his shoulders, puts the cup down on the counter, and introduces me as "the cake artist" to a bunch of kids in a circle, who are dying to know who I am. I set my cup down next to his as he keeps me close to him, his arm and shoulder touching mine the whole time. He brags to everyone how talented I am, being Mrs. Sparacini's apprentice and all. I go along with the lie. Realizing I'm stuck here and can't leave without making an ass out of myself, I make a short list of why I shouldn't run like hell:

1. Howie's the first person who makes me laugh like I used to with Francesca.
2. Howie gets cuter by the minute.
3. He smells like heaven.
4. Howie makes me think there's a chance my life could get better.

After I make my list, I glance over at the clock, thinking about the early morning.

He notices me checking the time. "Before it gets too late, let me show you the art."

"Sure."

Howie pulls me out of the kitchen and through a dining room, which leads to a living room, through a mini bar, which leads to a second living room, and then to a dark, wood-paneled door. He puts his finger up to his lips like we're five years old and sneaking around the house where we shouldn't be.

He swings the door open and gestures for me to walk into an enormous room filled with tiny paned windows on one side, solid dark wood walls with three abstract paintings hanging on the other. Another wall is lined with bookcases all the way up to a freakishly tall ceiling, complete with a ladder attached by a brass railing. I can smell the leather sofas and chairs perched on top of a huge multi-colored rug, probably handmade in some far-off foreign land. Howie closes the door.

I avoid looking at him. He scares me, this scares me, but at the same time I don't want to leave. I'm so messed up.

"Wow. This room is amazing." I need to fill the bubble of silence.

Howie walks up to me and reaches for the necklaces I'm clutching in the palm of my hand. He drapes each one over my head while he stares at my lips. He's totally got a kiss on his mind and I sooo don't know what to do about it.

So I turn away and walk along the wall of books, touching the spine of each one with my fingers, wondering what lurks inside the pages, wondering if someone became so torn apart by a story she'd decide to never take a chance on reading that kind of book again.

Howie stands in front of me. "Best room in the house, don't you think?"

I want to run like there's a grizzly bear chasing me.

"So you've known Z-man forever then?" I ask.

He smiles, "Forever, since kindergarten."

My armpits get hot. I hope I don't faint. Through the corner of my eye I see the lights from outside flickering through the windowpanes. He's about to kiss me. I know it. He leans into me a little bit.

I quickly turn my head, like when I'm at the doctor and he hits my knee with the rubber hammer thing and my leg jerks up.

"Carmella," Hannah yells. "Are you in there?"

Bang. The door flies open.

Howie and I jump. We spin around towards the doorway.

Hannah cups her hand over her mouth. "Oops. Sorry," she laughs. "We gotta go. Z-man says everyone out. It's almost curfew." She taps her wrist, laughing. She dashes out of the room like a kid.

Howie and I smile at each other, looking down at the ground, knowing she thinks she interrupted a kiss that never happened.

He clears his throat. "I guess we gotta go. I could give you a ride home if you want. I'm designated driver."

"No, no. I mean, I have a ride. She's driving. Well, no." Then reality hits me. I'll probably never see him again. "Well, maybe. You sure?"

"Yeah, totally," he says with a smile.

"Okay. But I live so far."

"I don't think you're far from here," Howie says.

By the time we get to the foyer, I'm not sure if I'm doing the right thing. Everyone from the party's walking past us, making a quick mass exit, like they've all done this before. We spot Jeremy and the girls. I tell the girls Jeremy and Howie are giving me a ride home. Madison shoots me a dirty look, and I'm terrified she's going to say something about Francesca. She's got wicked jealousy in her eyes.

"What's this thing?" Izzy asks as she points to a little metal oblong box attached to the inside of the doorframe. "Is this some weird language?" She gets her nose right up to it, other kids knocking into her as they walk by.

"You're kidding, right?" Howie says to Izzy.

Angry, drunk Madison tries to put her hand on her hip but misses. "Kidding about what?" She moves to snatch the box off the doorframe.

"Hey," Jeremy says. "What do you think you're doing?"

"I'm takin' the Christmas decorations off. Honestly, some people are so God damn lazy!"

Jeremy and Howie laugh. "It's a Mezuzah," Howie blurts. "You've never seen one of these? It blesses the house. The custom was started by a rabbi, who gave it to a king, who ..."

"Dude. Not time for Hebrew lessons," Jeremy says.

"C'mon, Mello, let's go," Madison slurs. She waves her arm at me.

"I'm going with them." I point.

Hannah walks out the door and down the steps, flinging her keys, "Designated sober driver is leaving. Let's go. We expect details, Mello."

Izzy pulls Madison by the sleeve, still laughing and stumbling.

Howie, Jeremy and I walk over to Howie's car.

Jeremy holds the front passenger door open with his arm stretched out as if he's a limo driver or something.

"Ms. …" Jeremy stands up straight and starts laughing. "Hey, I don't even know your last name."

"D'Agostino."

I slide into the front seat. Howie gets in. Jeremy jumps in the back seat.

Jeremy sits up and holds onto the headrest. "I know an awesome restaurant in the city called D'Agostino's. They got the best pizza. Your family own it?"

I twist around to face Jeremy. "Mine? No. My family owns a restoration and disaster recovery business, though. My grandfather started the business back in the fifties."

"What's the name?" Howie asks.

"Perfection Restoration."

"Haven't heard of it. But Carmella D'Agostino sounds like an Italian opera." Howie starts singing at the top of his lungs.

Jeremy sits back and shakes his head. "Every day I drive to school with him and put up with this shit."

"He sounds pretty good," I say.

Howie belts out some fake Italian opera song as he turns the corner.

Jeremy laughs. "I know. He gets cast in every production. I think he has a bright future in theatre." Jeremy puts his finger up to his lips. "But he won't listen to me. His parents have him brainwashed into going to med school."

"I'm in the car, you know," Howie says as he turns the wheel.

Howie and Jeremy ask me questions about growing up in Elmwood Park, going to Catholic schools all my life and how I met Anna. I ask both of them questions about growing up Jewish, living in Glencoe, and how they met. Then we compare schools and classes.

"So Sunday's the big birthday party," I say to Jeremy once we're in my neighborhood. "Are you doing it at your house or somewhere else?"

Jeremy drums his fingers on his knees. "House party. A magician is coming."

"Sounds like fun. Howie said you help plan all the birthdays."

"Yeah, well, my bro and I plan them together. It's the highlight of his year."

"He's lucky to have a brother like you."

"I bet you'd do the same thing," Jeremy says.

John Lennon's "Losin' You" from *Double Fantasy* echoes through the car.

I turn to Howie. "You like John Lennon?"

"Yeah … doesn't everyone?" he asks.

Jeremy nods his head. "Totally."

"I love him. I used to spend my entire weekends playing, I mean, listening to his music." My hands flail.

"So you play an instrument?" Howie asks.

I'm not going to tell these guys the truth, they'd never understand. I don't even understand. When Francesca moved in with Donny, I got sick of dealing with everyone at school, even Anna. So I hung out with Francesca and Donny, wrote songs and played my guitar nonstop. I'll tell them half the truth. I can't go near my guitar without hyperventilating now and I'm sure I'll never play again.

"I meant I used to play around with writing songs."

"Songwriter, huh?" Howie smiles and nods.

We pull up into my driveway. "This is your house, right?" Howie asks.

"Yeah."

I look over at the pine tree in the corner of the front yard Dad and I nursed back to health one spring after it lost a lot of needles because of some fungus, the porch light we never turn on, and the cedar siding my parents have repainted by the youth group at church to raise money every five years. Other families have basketball hoops in their front yards and swing sets in the back. We don't. My reality. I wonder what Howie's house looks like.

"I'll walk you in," Howie says.

As we walk up the sidewalk, Howie says, "Hey, since you're obviously a huge John Lennon fan, you headed to the exhibit this weekend?"

My heart stops. "No, I thought they were all sold out."

"You mean you're a huge fan of John Lennon and you didn't get tickets?"

I want to shout at Howie I didn't get tickets to the *Bed-In for Peace Exhibit* because I was making funeral arrangements. My heart thumps so hard I wonder if my neck is bulging.

"I would have gotten them but I forgot. I had a lot going on." I want to tell him I just lost my sister, but he'll start asking questions, and I don't want to go against Dad. Besides, if I told him, I'd be the girl whose sister died of a drug overdose, instead of just a girl. A girl he might even like.

"You should come with me then. I got an extra ticket for Sunday."

"Really?"

"I'll call you."

"Okay."

"Catch you later." Howie steps forward like he might give me a hug, or a kiss, but I step back and give him a three-year-old wave.

I open the front door with my key and walk in without turning back.

***

I take my coat off. My father's in the kitchen rummaging through the fridge, fork in hand, in search of his usual midnight snack. He pulls out a plastic container with a green lid.

"You're late." My father shoves a bite of cold lasagna into his mouth.

"I was at a party." I hang up my coat in the front closet. "I went with Anna's friends. Where's Mom?"

My mother walks down the steps, still holding onto the railing. She's exhausted.

She walks up to me, the phone in her shaky hand. "We've been calling you all night but you've been ignoring our calls. You're never out this late. I thought something happened to you."

I pull my phone out of my purse. It's out of battery.

"Sorry. I didn't know my phone was out. I didn't mean for you to worry."

"Anna drive you home?" My father grabs a paper towel and wipes his mouth.

"Um, no. Anna didn't go. She was pissed about losing her game. So I went with her friends."

No way am I telling Mom and Dad about Howie. They'd totally freak out. I've never dated before and I'm sure they'd go nuts, hire some private investigator to follow me if they thought I was interested in a guy. They never cared what I did before, but now Francesca's gone and I'm under a gigantic microscope.

"The first time you're out past curfew and your phone dies? Don't do this to me, Carmella. You're always so responsible. You're the one I never had to worry about," my mother says, her eyes glassy.

"Sorry. I'm only twenty minutes late. It won't happen again." I want to tell her she never had to worry about me because I never left the house before.

My mother crosses her arms in front of her and shakes her head.

I remember Howie's invite to the John Lennon exhibit. Since they'll totally freak over me going out with a guy, and never understand me wanting to go to the exhibit, I lie.

"So, the girls were talking about going to a movie Sunday afternoon."

"You can't go," my mother says.

"Why? I'll do my homework in the morning."

My mother takes a deep breath. She looks like she's in pain.

"What's wrong?" I ask.

"Go ahead, tell her," my dad says before shoving another bite of lasagna in his mouth.

My mother rolls her eyes. "Your father and I—"

"You mean *you*," my father mumbles in between chewing.

"Okay, *I* was thinking we all need some help dealing with everything, so we're going as a family Sunday afternoon to speak to Father Gonzalez about a mission trip."

"A mission trip?"

"Yes, over spring break. I don't know where, yet. Probably Mexico, or Haiti."

Is she nuts? Why would I want to go to some poor village in the middle of nowhere? This might help her, but not me. I wonder where we'd sleep. Shower?

"Where would we sleep?"

"In a church."

"You mean, like on the pews or on the floor?"

"We'll bring sleeping bags."

"What about showers and going to the bathroom?"

"No showers, but there's one bathroom."

"One bathroom? For how many people?"

"Twenty or so."

"No way. I am not sharing a bathroom with twenty strangers."

"A trip like this will make us appreciate our life. We need to reach out and help other people. Father says these trips help people heal their wounds."

"Why can't we go to Florida for spring break, like normal people?" I ask.

"We certainly don't need to sit on a beach and indulge ourselves. What we need to do is give back and feel closer to God."

I want to scream at my mother I don't want or need to go where people live in mud huts. I don't want to go somewhere I can't shower for a week and am forced to sleep on the floor with a bunch of strangers. But her eyes are so puffy, her wrinkles much deeper, and she doesn't stand up straight anymore.

What I want to do is tell her I noticed when Francesca started eighth grade our whole family changed and I don't know why. The three of them fought so much, I can't remember when they weren't yelling at each other. But why bother? She won't hear me anyhow.

My mother walks towards me. She tightens the belt to her robe and sniffs.

"I paced the floor worried you were dead somewhere for an hour. Then I called Anna and she had no idea where the party was. This is not like you. I suppose you were drinking too."

"No."

"You smell like beer."

"It was a crowded party and people were drinking beer and breathing on me all over the place. Someone spilled on me. I had a pop, I swear."

"This is what I'm talking about. What happened to Francesca is starting to happen to you."

"I'm not Francesca." My arms stiffen up.

"We're not talking about Francesca." My father rubs his forehead. "We're talking about you and we decided you should come work for us."

"What? I go out once in like two years, come home a little late and you're gonna punish me?"

"This isn't a punishment." My dad rinses the dirty plastic container and pulls the top rack of the dishwasher open. "Your mother and I decided a few days ago you should come to work with us. We were going to tell you tomorrow."

I go and do something other than play my guitar and sit at Francesca's apartment and my parents have completely flipped out. "I have a job. You're telling me to quit the bakery and work for you? Francesca never wanted to learn the business, why do I have to?"

"Carmella, we're trying to help." My mother walks closer to me, her eyebrows crunched up.

"Help what? I can't believe this. Why are you treating me like you don't trust me?"

"We know you've been through a lot and we're worried about you. You're out way later than you ever were before. Your cell phone conveniently runs out of battery ... Carmella, you're going to end up like Francesca if we don't watch what you're doing," my mother says.

"Why are you two acting so crazy?"

My father rubs his nose, takes a deep breath and crosses his arms. "We're not crazy. We want to make sure nothing happens to you. First you go visit Donny in the city, then instead of coming home with Anna, you go to a party where kids are drinking. It's not like you to abandon your best friend. Anna would never go to a party with people she just met."

My father has never said anything like this to me. I've always been the one he could count on to do the right thing. I won't dare tell him I didn't want to go to the game with Howie and Jeremy in the first place, this night was all Anna's idea. And then she ditched me. Forget it. I feel like we're playing Monopoly and Francesca quit and I have to take her place. I'm stuck being the shoe. Francesca was always the shoe when she and I played.

Ten minutes ago, I was on top of the world. I thought maybe I could get out of the black hole I fell into, but now, I feel like giving up. I can't go to the John Lennon exhibit. I can't even think about seeing Howie again. And the bakery was the only thing I had to look forward to. My parents are all twisted inside and out. I can't handle fighting with them like Francesca did. The thought of a mission trip is making me sick. Maybe if I agree to work for Perfection they will stop worrying about me and won't make me go away to some poor country. If I go work for them, we won't fight.

"So, if I quit the bakery and go work for Perfection, can we forget about the mission trip?"

My mother tilts her head. "I don't know. But we're going to talk to Father on Sunday anyhow."

***

I crawl into bed. I wish I could talk to Francesca. I plug my phone into the charger. Fifty text messages from Anna pop up, twenty of them apologizing for not going to the party, the rest wondering how it was and wanting to hear all the details, hoping we can still do a double date with Howie and Jeremy.

I text her back: *can't see howie ever again long story.* What I'd like to tell her is this is all her fault. If she had gone to the stupid party with me, my parents wouldn't have freaked out. Tomorrow I'll text her and tell her I want to be alone for the rest of my life, i.e., don't want to ever speak to her again.

I toss and turn and try to go to sleep, but I can't get Howie out of my mind. I open my eyes and stare at my guitar, still sitting in its stand, still untouched since the night I got the news, its hourglass outline shining from the light of the same moon I was standing under with Howie a few hours ago.

I roll over and wonder if Howie's sleeping and what he'll do tomorrow, or the rest of his life. I check the red numbers on my clock, and instead of dreading the thought of Francesca showing up, I pray for Francesca to come sit at the end of my bed. I would love to talk to her about Mom and Dad, how I feel like I don't know who they are and I wish I knew what to do to make all this better.

As I stare up at the ceiling of my bedroom, waiting for Francesca, I make a list.

What I lost in one night

1. The cutest guy ever, who wants to go to John Lennon exhibits with me.
2. A job I like.
3. A best friend.
4. A father and mother who trust me.

Chapter 7

Reasons why my life sucks and keeps getting worse by the minute

1. I refuse to accept Anna's apology. Not going to the party with me, not being able to think past her stupid volleyball game, she royally let me down.
2. My father walks around like he's got an alien from another planet living inside of him. Like his body is here but he's been abducted from earth.
3. My mother's an emotional mess. She tries to act like everything's okay but she's nervous as hell, drops things and her hands shake all the time.
4. Going to school is going to be torture without Anna as a friend.

I check the time. Two in the afternoon and I still haven't told Mrs. Sparacini that I need to quit. The bakery's been crazy-busy, as usual for a Saturday morning. While she was working on the Lombardo wedding cake, which turned out to be one of her best ever, I took care of all the customers. Some of them come in every Saturday, like Giovanni and Rocco. They're about ninety years old and always order biscotti and coffee and sit in the table over in the corner and talk for hours. They remind me of how Francesca and I used to spend so much time together and make me wish we had a chance to be old ladies, talking over coffee every Saturday.

When Mrs. Sparacini got back a while ago from delivering the Lombardo cake, I tried to tell her about quitting, but she seemed too stressed out about starting on a cake for some firehouse chief she'd agreed to do last minute. Mrs. Sparacini said men don't ever plan ahead and a fire chief deserves a big, beautiful cake honoring his sixtieth birthday no matter what.

Howie texted me about the John Lennon exhibit this morning. I texted him back and told him I couldn't go tomorrow because I had to study for an exam. No way could I tell him I need to go talk to a priest with my parents about some crazy mission trip.

Mrs. Sparacini's at the worktable, frosting the cake. I dread telling her I have to quit, but my mother's already planned to pick me up from school next Monday and bring me to their office so I have to tell her today. I want to give her time to find my replacement.

Saturday afternoons when we're not busy, I put away a lot of supplies. As I put each box of sugar and flour on the shelf, I think about Howie. I think about what my life was like last week. I had Anna as a friend and Howie was in here with Jeremy, making jokes and flirting. Last Monday, I thought my life couldn't get any worse. I reach for my phone to call Francesca and vent and put it back in my apron pocket. I remember she won't answer.

I rip open a carton of cleaning supplies and my phone bings in my pocket. Since noon the girls have been texting me. Hannah wants more details, Izzy thinks this Howie thing is so exciting, nobody dates guys from the north suburbs. And Madison is positive the kiss with Howie—which they're all assuming happened, but never did—

was a one-time deal for me. She's convinced Howie was using me for the night. I text back to them: *stop texting me i'm working.*

"Carmella," Mrs. Sparacini says.

Her voice makes me jump a little.

"You seem distracted today, like something's on your mind." Her eyes are glued to the hydrant she's molding. "You need some time off? I can get my sister-in-law to help out for a few weeks again." Mrs. Sparacini stops what she's doing and winks at me.

"Thanks, Mrs. Sparacini. Actually, I need to talk to you about something." I rub my forehead, doom overwhelming me. "I don't think I can work here anymore." The words get stuck in my throat.

"Say no more," Mrs. Sparacini says. "My sister-in-law will help me. Take as much time as you need. Call when you're up to coming back."

"Thanks, Mrs. Sparacini. I'm not sure when I'll be back though." I watch her make flames out of frosting, not able say out loud that I'll never be back.

"No problem," she says. "Take as much time as you need."

***

A few hours later, Mrs. Sparacini finishes the five layered cake, each one a square. Small houses, buildings, fire trucks, hoses and hydrants rest on each layer. She takes a few photographs. She insists on delivering all her cakes herself in her little delivery van, so I'll handle the trickle of customers that will come in while she's gone. It's nearly five, the slowest part of the day.

I hear the jingle of the front door as I turn the water on to do some dishes. In a huff, I turn the water off, dry my hands and slap through the swinging door.

Howie's in front of the cookie case. With a girl.

Twisting the towel as hard as I can, I try to take a breath. I think I got punched in the stomach.

"Hi," Howie pops up. His voice cracks a little. The girl stares at me.

I play with my necklaces, hoping my neck isn't red or my eyeballs haven't fallen out or maybe I'm peeing on myself and don't know it. How could he? Figures. Madison was right.

"Carmella, I want you to meet Stacey," Howie says.

Stacey smiles.

She's got long straight dark hair. Crystal blue eyes. Skinny legs. She's wearing yogas. Figures he'd go for the skinny type.

"Nice to meet you." I rub one sweaty palm onto my white apron and squeeze the towel again as I park myself in front of the cookie counter, shielding myself. I try not to make eye contact with Howie.

Howie's hair is wet and he's dressed in sweat shorts. Cute. They must have worked out together.

He smiles at me. "A friend of Stacey's is turning sixteen and she needs some cupcakes."

"I'm not sure if Mrs. Sparacini makes cupcakes anymore."

Mrs. Sparacini makes anything for anyone, but I'm ticked off and don't want to sell cupcakes to Howie's skinny friend. She probably won't eat them anyway.

"Oh." Howie's smile fades. "That's too bad. We drove all the way here from the rink in Winnetka because I convinced my cousin this is the best bakery in the Chicago area. I thought you did everything here."

"Cousin?" I turn my head towards Stacey.

Her eyes bulge. "Are you serious? You can't make cupcakes?"

"Oh, sure. I was joking." I practically sprint to the register and grab an order form, my armpits burning up. Stacey does an over the top eye roll before she rattles off some details. She wants three different kinds, devil's food, red velvet and carrot, each with fun frostings to match and some sprinkles, nuts or confetti on top. Her phone starts playing Lady Gaga's "Bad Romance." She laughs, starts texting, and walks away.

Howie rakes the top of his head with his fingers and leans in towards me.

I don't know what to say so I blurt out the first thing that comes to mind. "So you two workout or what?"

"Stacey and I skate."

"Oh yeah, you did mention a rink. So you're a hockey player," I say.

"No, figure."

A bomb goes off in my brain.

Howie immediately points to me. "You've got that look, and I'm telling you, I'm not what you think. I mean, I'm not gay."

"Oh, well, I mean, there aren't many, and well, so she's your partner? Like those pair skaters in the Olympics?"

"No, although my coach would like me to do pairs, I'm strictly solo. I'm going to Nationals in a few months."

"Oh, wow. You been skating since you were born or what?"

"Pretty much. Hey, sorry you can't make the John Lennon exhibit tomorrow."

"Yeah, brutal exam, you know?"

"Chemistry you said?"

"Yep, not my thing." I totally lie.

No way am I going to tell Howie the truth.

Howie points to a black and white photograph of Mrs. Sparacini and her parents hanging on the wall behind me.

"They mob related?" Howie raises his eyebrows.

"No, not mob related." I laugh. "That's Mrs. Sparacini and her parents when they opened this place. She's the little girl in between them."

Howie laughs. "Oh, right."

I want to jump out the window. I'm dying to tell him I'm so glad he came in, I'm so excited to see him, I've been thinking about him every hour since I left him last night. But I choke on fear. Fear of Howie barging into my life, then tossing me aside for someone else when he finds out what kind of person I am, how I let people down who count on me. Howie seems a little nervous too.

"Can we go now, Howe? I got stuff to do. Do this flirty thing on your own watch." Stacey keeps texting.

Howie clears his throat. "So, I was wondering if you want to catch a movie next weekend?"

My heart explodes into tiny pieces, like a Jackson Pollock painting. "I'd love to."

I think about my life. "But I can't."

"Maybe another weekend then?"

"No, no. I … I can't, ever."

Howie's face drops. "Is this some private school Catholic thing? Can't date 'til you're thirty?"

For a second, I almost blurt out I'm kidding, yes I'll go out with you. But the disaster list—aka my life—is totally out of control and getting worse. I'm the one note that is so off key, I'll wreck the whole song. I can't go out with Howie. I can't.

I close my eyes. I should have done it a second ago. "I'm sorry. I have a boyfriend."

"Funny. You're kidding again, right?"

I tilt my head towards the floor.

"Okay. I knew it. The good ones are always taken." Howie flips his keys and walks backwards.

Howie smiles at me, "Hey listen, if things don't work out, call me. Consider me your back up plan."

I scrunch my nose up, holding back my smile.

"Howie, we are so out of here." Stacey pulls Howie by the arm.

Howie waves, "Till next time, Mello. I'm serious. Call me or text me as soon as you dump the boyfriend." Howie puts his hand up to his ear, then does a thing like he's texting me. Stacey shoves him out the door.

As he and Stacey walk past the front window, I'm dying to run after him, dying to tell him the truth. But instead, I pick up Stacey's order and walk back to the office.

I set the order down on Mrs. Sparacini's desk. Her office light is off, and standing there, I realize seeing Howie is like finding the stupid lamp in the dark, when no one is home and I search for the light and when I finally turn it on, the empty feeling of being so alone, the freak-out feeling that a burglar is in the house—all of those bad feelings go away.

My mouth waters and I taste blood. I've chewed the inside of my cheek so hard I'm bleeding.

Chapter 8

Reasons why Oreos and milkshakes are my new best friends

1. They help me forget the bad stuff.
2. They help me remember the good stuff.
3. I can be myself when I'm with them.
4. They don't try and control me.
5. They don't judge me.

November

I stuff my Oreos into my messenger bag and head to the Wendy's for a chocolate Frosty. Since I don't drive home after school with Anna anymore, a six-pack of Oreos and an extra large is my routine on the days Mom doesn't pick me up and take me over to Perfection. The guy at the Shell station in the glass box must think I'm a crazy person obsessed with Oreos. Tomorrow I'll hit the grocery store and buy the industrial size so I can avoid him. Besides, the six-pack doesn't cut it anymore. An hour after I get home I'm searching the kitchen for something to eat. Lately the only thing I can find are chocolate chips that have turned patchy white from last time my mother baked cookies—for my fourteenth birthday—or mini Marshmallows left over from last year's Thanksgiving's sweet potato casserole.

I dip my Oreo into the Frosty, wondering who invented the fingerless glove, about the only thing I'm thankful for right now. Thanksgiving's next week and I'm counting down the days as if I'm preparing myself for a beating. This will be our first holiday without Francesca, and I'm not sure if I'll survive. Thanksgiving was her favorite holiday because it wasn't a two-day deal with the family and we didn't have to suffer through another white elephant present exchange, where one of us was guaranteed to come home with a pea green pleather wallet Grandma found in her basement from the sixties.

I step over the crack in the sidewalk and adjust the strap on my shoulder, an Oreo between my teeth. I dread the thought of another holiday at Grandma's without Francesca. Even though she ditched out on family holidays last year, I figured she'd be back with us this year, but now she'll never be with us. She'll never be around to tell me to ignore all the gushing about cousin Tony at the table, or it doesn't matter we're always the understudies of the play who never get a chance to prove ourselves worthy of the lead. I will sit alone at the table forever, without Francesca's exaggerated eye rolls to distract me while I'm forced to listen to how wonderful Tony is, how he gets such good grades. Aunt Maria will go on and on about how Tony's a senior this year and quarterback of the football team. Then she'll remind us this is the second year in a row he's made captain, as if we couldn't count. She likes to be sure everyone keeps track of how perfect her Tony is. She'll squeal, "We're sooo proud of you, Tony."

Yick. I chomp down on the Oreo, the crunchy chocolate bits and cold creamy Frosty swirling around in my mouth. Now I'll be wiping dishes in the corner of Grandma's kitchen without Francesca's smart-ass jokes in my ear, and I won't be going upstairs to hide out in Grandma's pink bathroom so Francesca can give me her "it doesn't matter who they want you to be, you need to be yourself" lecture while she blows cigarette smoke out the window.

"Carmella."

I turn my head. Donny's in a silver four-door car. He yells at me through the window. The Oreo slips out of my fingers a little.

I start to run, but my penny loafers are too loose. I'm juggling a Frosty and the cookies and my bag. I think I'm screwed. So I do some wicked speed walking and ignore him.

"Carmella. Hey, stop."

If I could wear what I wanted to wear to school, I'd be wearing my army boots. I'd dump the Frosty and cookies and run like hell to get away from Donny. I'd make an easy escape.

I glance over my shoulder but don't spot the car Donny was driving anywhere. He's probably gone, but I keep up the pace. I'm not taking any chances.

"Carmella."

Shit. He's walking right behind me. "Leave me alone. I'm not speaking to you."

Donny yanks my arm back, I spill my Frosty all over my hand, all over the sidewalk.

"Damn it."

"Sorry. Here, let me help you."

"I don't need your help." I run to the garbage can and toss the Frosty in, my glove covered in milkshake. I hold on tight to the three Oreos in my left hand.

"Why are you following me? What do you want?"

"I want to talk to you, so I thought I'd catch you coming out of school."

"I'm not at school, so technically you're stalking me and I don't want to ever speak to you again after what you said about me and Francesca, so leave me alone."

Donny turns around and walks away.

Relieved, I continue through the village green park. My heart races and my fingers squeeze the Oreos tight. If he thinks I'm ever going to speak to him again, he's crazy, and especially now. I have no clue how I'm going to get through the next week of my life without some vital organ like my heart or brain bursting or shutting down on me. I can't sleep, and Francesca is showing up every other night at the end of my bed. And now the thought of facing the holidays with out her? Wacked.

I wish Dad would agree to Mom's idea. She suggested going down to the city for Thanksgiving, just the three of us, I thought, wow, what an awesome idea. Maybe my parents are changing. Maybe we can go back to life as a normal family, where we actually want to spend time together and we can talk to each other without it turning into a fight. Like how things were before Francesca's life started going to hell.

"Here." Donny shoves a few napkins at my hand.

My feet fly out of my loafers. My head whips around.

"Sorry. Didn't mean to terrorize you."

"Shit."

I snatch the napkins out of Donny's hand and start wiping the sticky goo off, wishing I had my Frosty back. I decide to give him the silent treatment. Donny surprises me. He's all cleaned up, his face has color, like he's healthy. He's showered and he's got an overcoat on instead of his usual leather jacket. I put my shoe back on and continue my speed walk.

"Listen, Carmella, I need to talk to you. Okay. So ignore me. Fine. I know you can hear me."

I toss the Oreos into a garbage can and stuff my hands into my pockets. I don't dare tell Donny I think he looks much better than he did when I saw him last time at the bar.

"I'll buy you another milkshake or whatever you want. It's cold as shit out here and I think you're nuts for drinking milkshakes, but could you stop for one second and listen to me?"

I twirl my fingers in my pockets, the damp chill in the air and the grey sky a perfect backdrop to the scene where I turn around and punch Donny in the nose.

"Carmella, c'mon. I'm sorry I was an asshole. I was trying to help you understand Francesca. She was hurting all the time. She was always trying to protect you."

I'm mad as hell at Donny, but the tone in his voice makes me wonder if he's suffering like I am. I wonder if he dreads getting out of bed in the morning and if he spends most of his day in a fantasy about climbing back in. I wonder if Donny gets the same weird feeling as I do, where all of a sudden, out of nowhere, I'm slapped in the chest, like if I saw my dog get hit by a car and fly across the road, his head splattered all over the pavement. It hurts so bad I want to fall to the ground and curl up in a ball and stay there until the pain goes away. I wonder if Donny ever aches like that.

"Did you hear what I said?"

I stop and turn around. "No, I didn't."

"I said I'm recovering. I'm clean and sober and I'm on the ninth step."

"Yeah, so?"

"The ninth step is to make amends with people you've hurt and I hurt you."

Donny's words paint over the black in my life. I'm desperate to talk to him about Francesca, desperate to connect with another human being who can understand how hard it is to live without my big sister.

***

Donny and I walk into the Elmwood coffee house, down the street from Mrs. Sparacini's bakery. A short woman with a sharp accent, bright red lipstick, puffy jet-black hair, and large, square, red-rimmed glasses comes over to the counter. She grips the sides of the cash register.

"What can I get for you?"

"I would like a venti frappacino, please."

Donny orders coffee, black.

We find a small table in the corner, next to the window.

I squeeze my hands together and tap my feet on the floor. I can't think of anything to say. Donny seems like a new person.

"So how are you?" Donny asks.

"Fine."

"You don't seem fine."

"How do you know?"

"I can just tell."

I adjust the rolled waistband of my skirt. It's pinching my stomach. I'm all bloated and not finding my new fat suit very comfortable. I wonder if Donny notices the ten pounds I gained in the last month.

"So you're all different, all cleaned up. You stopped drinking and everything?"

"Yep."

"How's your friend Anna?" he asks.

"Fine."

I rip open the straw.

"Really?"

"Yeah."

"And the bakery?"

"Fine."

I stab the straw into the frappacino and gulp some down.

"You still having dreams about her?"

I sit back and cross my arms, afraid to tell him the truth, but I do anyway.

"Yeah."

"I can tell. You've got dark circles under your eyes and they look a little puffy."

I know Donny means *I* seem puffy.

"Maybe you should talk to someone. Ever think about a grief support group?"

"My parents are forcing me to see a shrink," I lie. I don't want Donny to know how my life is getting worse and lately, I'm totally sure God put me on this earth to suffer.

"How's that going?"

"Great."

"Wow. Everything's freakin' fantastic then?"

"Yep."

I pinch the straw and gulp down the frappacino.

Donny sips his coffee and leans back.

"Wow, I'm surprised," he says.

"Why?"

"I figured you would have some trouble dealing, that's all. I must have had you and Francesca all wrong."

"What are you talking about?"

"I figured you'd be in agony, missing her so bad, like your world was crashing in on you because that's how I feel. Some days, I can barely get out of bed in the morning. And every day, I'm dying for a drink, for an upper or downer to take the pain away. But you? You seem to be completely in control of your life, as if nothing's happened. I guess she didn't mean so much to you."

"You are such an asshole."

I grab my messenger bag and start to slide off the chair, but I get stuck.

Donny doesn't try and stop me.

I push the chair out, the wooden leg scrapes the floor, and right when I stand up, my mouth waters, frappacino tickling the back of my throat. I cup my hand onto my mouth and run to the bathroom, hoping to God I don't puke all over the floor.

***

I rinse my mouth out for the hundredth time, wishing for a toothbrush and some toothpaste. I wipe my face with a white rough paper towel and walk out of the bathroom. I look over at the table. Donny's gone.

The puffy haired lady with the red lipstick shouts at me as I pass by the counter.

"Everything okay, hon?"

I nod without stopping, then pull the metal handle of the coffee shop door open, wishing Donny hadn't left, wishing I had another chance to tell him the truth. I stare down at the cracks and holes in the sidewalk. My stomach's all twisted inside out and back again. Why didn't I tell Donny the truth about how I felt? I wanted to, I just couldn't. Oh well. What good comes out of being honest and truthful anyhow? Truth is bullshit.

"Carmella."

I look up.

Donny's leaning on his car. "You okay? C'mon, I'll give you a ride home. We don't have to talk."

I don't say a word, but get in the car. I think a truck ran over me.

Donny's car is so clean, all shiny and brand new. "This yours?"

"No, my sponsor's."

"Sponsor?"

"Yeah. A sponsor is someone who helps addicts, like a mentor. Carmella, I'm sorry what I said about you and Francesca. I didn't mean to sound like an asshole."

"Yeah, well it was an asshole kind of comment."

"I know. I'm working on my delivery. I'm sorry, again. Can you forgive me?"

"No."

He looks super mad or hurt or both. "Why not?"

"Because you keep saying stuff that hurts my feelings."

"I'm trying to change."

"Well, go change with someone else."

"So you've never screwed up in your life?"

"What do *my* screw ups have to do with *your* screw ups?"

"People screw up, Carmella. So never forgive other people, and they won't forgive you, right? Is that the rule book you want to live by?"

I chew on my cheek. The back of my throat hurts. I focus on breathing because I think I stopped for a second. Truth is, I don't believe in forgiveness anymore since I lost Francesca.

I stare out the window. "I didn't make the rulebook. To be honest, I don't think people forgive each other, they just say they do. They lie."

Donny doesn't say anything. I expect him to argue with me, tell me I'm wrong, say I'm crazy for thinking these screwed up thoughts. I expect him to give me a solid argument about forgiveness. I've been told my whole life people forgive and forget, but I'm done believing in anyone or anything.

We turn into the neighborhood.

I wonder what he thinks about me. "If I accept your apology, do you get a gold star?"

"Not until I make amends to everyone I pissed off," he says.

"Okay, so cross me off the list. I forgive you."

"Nope."

"What? So now you're not *accepting* my *acceptance* of your apology?"

"Your apology has to be genuine. Not this *I'll forgive you so you get the hell away from me* shit."

"Arghh. I didn't say that."

"Yeah, well, I know you're thinking it."

"How do you know what I'm thinking?"

"Carmella, I might have been drunk and high most of the time, but I know you better than you think I do. And Francesca talked about you a lot, especially the last month. She really missed you."

"Why didn't she return my calls then? Why did she cut me off?"

Donny shakes his head. "I don't know. I asked her, but she'd just get all pissed off at me, tell me to mind my own business. If you want me to be honest, I'd say she was somehow protecting you."

I nod, believing him.

As Donny pulls into the driveway, I check out the pine tree in our front yard to make sure the needles aren't turning brown. I don't want it to get sick again.

"So what's the right way to forgive you?"

"Be real. Be true. Don't be angry." He smiles. "Say I forrrrgggiiivvvee you."

Donny's face makes me laugh. "Okay, okay. I ffffoooorrrrrgggiiivvvveee you."

"Great. Only ninety-nine other people left on the list."

"Thanks for the ride." I open the car door.

"Hey, keep seeing the shrink, and you need to start sleeping."

I nod.

"Carmella?"

"Yeah?"

"Make sure you don't hide from your life, like I did. And seriously, call me if you ever want to talk about Francesca or anything. I promise not to be an asshole."

"Really?"

"Yes, really."

When I get in the house, I head for the kitchen, straight for the stale chocolate chips. I reach into the bag and pull out a handful, but right before I stuff them into my mouth, I hear Donny's voice tell me not to hide from my life like he did. Every day he fights the urge to drink and do drugs. I walk over to the garbage can and toss out all the stale, gross chocolate chips.

***

Francesca's side of the room seems desperately cold and for the first time I'm a little freaked out by her bed. I can't fall asleep. I slide off my bed, trip over my shoes and nestle into the back of my closet. I sit down on the floor, the arms of my white uniform shirts covering my ears. I zip open Francesca's purse, pulling out pieces of her: her wallet, the rest of her mints, a pen. My eyes start to burn, so I push my shoes into the corner and pull a sweater out of my dirty clothes hamper and lie down, Francesca's purse in my arms.

I smell cigarette smoke. I sit straight up and my eyes fly open. My heart thumps in my fingertips. I stare at a shadow sitting in front of my bed. I fight to focus and adjust my eyes. The shadow, against the bed, looks like the outline of Francesca, her legs up and elbows resting on her knees.

I whisper, "Francesca."

"Time for change," she whispers back. "Be strong."

"I miss you," I say.

"Remember, I'm nowhere but everywhere at the same time. I promise to protect you."

"Francesca?" I blink.

She disappears.

Chapter 9

Reasons why I want to skip Thanksgiving

1. I've got nothing to be thankful for.
2. It was Francesca's favorite holiday.
3. It will be the first time I see everyone in my family since the funeral.
4. Holidays are torture when the one person who used to help me get through them is gone.
5. **I'd rather sit in my closet and forget about it.**

I pour a glass of orange juice and sit down at the kitchen table. My mother's got her head in the cabinet next to the stove. Cans of pumpkin, blocks of cream cheese, measuring cups, bags of sugar and flour are scattered around the countertops, a sure sign she's making pumpkin cheesecake, Francesca's favorite Thanksgiving dessert. Last year, when Francesca refused to come to Thanksgiving, Mom made the cheesecake anyhow. No one in the family touched the cheesecake, so I brought the whole thing over to Francesca and Donny's place the next day. The three of us had our own Tombstone pizza Thanksgiving.

My mother pours the graham crackers into a zip bag and I can't decide if I should pity her or write her off as a lunatic. The thought of the stupid cheesecake, sitting in the middle of Grandma's dining room table, seems borderline nuts.

"You know no one's going to eat that thing."

"What?"

"The cheesecake. No one will go near it."

"Why do you say that?" My mother picks up the rolling pin and whacks at the graham crackers.

"Because no one even touched the cheesecake last year."

She rolls the pin over the crackers, turning them into fine crumbs. "They were saving it for her last year."

"So this year, we'll all dig in, like some celebration thing?"

My mother stands up straight, still gripping the rolling pin with her left hand. "Of course not."

"Then why are you doing this?"

"Because every year I make cheesecake. Why is this such a big deal? It's cheesecake, Carmella." She flings her arm up in the air.

"Every year the cheesecake is barely eaten. You made it for Francesca because she never ate the pumpkin pie Aunt Maria made or Grandma's apple pie. When she didn't come to Thanksgiving last year, you still made it. I think you're crazy for doing this."

"We'll take the cheesecake to the office then."

I glance around at the mess in the kitchen and put a piece of graham cracker crumb on my tongue.

"Where's Dad?"

"At the office."

"On Thanksgiving?"

"He had work to catch up on."

"He hasn't taken a day off since the funeral. He used to at least be home on Sundays and holidays."

"Things got busy, that's all."

I don't know how she carries on as though everything's the same. I can't act as though nothing's happened. We're not the same and we never will be. I can't do this holiday.

I put my elbow up on the table and straighten up. "I'm not going."

Mom lifts the Ziplock up to see if the crumbs are crushed enough. "Go where?"

"To Grandma's."

She puts the bag down. "Don't be silly. It's Thanksgiving, our first holiday."

"Exactly why I'm not going."

She pours the crumbs into a glass-mixing bowl. "Carmella, I understand. This is hard for all of us."

"Yeah, so count me out."

"You don't have a choice."

"Why not?"

"Because we're a family. We need to be together." My mother pours melted butter into the graham cracker mix and starts mixing.

"Why am I always the one who gives in?"

She stops and huffs. "What are you talking about?"

"You wanted to go into the city for Thanksgiving, just the three of us. I thought that sounded like a good idea, but Dad didn't want to go, so we're not going. You want to go on this stupid mission trip, so we're going. You guys wanted me to quit my job at the bakery and come work for you, so I did. Why can't I ever do what I want to do?"

"Carmella, I can't fight anymore. You and your father are tearing me apart." My mother scrapes the sides of the bowl with the fork.

She pours the mixture into the pan and smashes it down with her fist. "Be ready by two, that's when your father will be home."

I get up from the table. "I'm not going and you can't make me."

She stops. "Carmella, make your father happy, make me happy, make the rest of the family happy. Why is that so hard to for you to do lately?"

"Because maybe I'm sick of you and Dad telling me what to do all the time. I have nothing to be thankful for and I don't want to go celebrate. For once I want to do what I want. And maybe I'm sick of living my life like you do, for everyone else."

My mother's eyes fill with tears. "Don't you dare talk to me like that."

I can't believe those words came out of my mouth.

My mother keeps pounding the crust with her fist.

Almost to the steps, I turn around. "Why does Dad have to be with family every single holiday? Why can't just the three of us be together for once?"

"Carmella, your father wants to be around his family right now."

"Yeah? Well, what about what I want? Why can't we ever do anything alone? Everything we do is always with other people. We used to go on a summer vacation every year. Why did we stop?"

My mother unwraps the cream cheese, her movements slow and deliberate. Without looking at me she continues to work. "Carmella, I don't know anything anymore and I'm tired."

***

At one thirty, my father comes through the front door. My mother is up in her room getting dressed. I'm still in my pajamas. At two o'clock, my mother yells from the kitchen "time to go." I lock my door, crawl into the closet and slide the door closed.

My mother knocks. "Carmella. Please open the door. Let's go."

I wrap Francesca's favorite shirt around my ears.

"Carmella." My father's voice bellows from the kitchen. "Where is she?"

My heart starts to pound fast.

"She's in her room," my mother says. She's standing outside my door, jiggling the knob. "Please, Carmella. Don't do this. I'm not going to sit at the holiday table childless."

My mother starts crying.

"God damn it, Carmella." My father's voice gets closer. The lock pings and my father storms into my room.

I sit up, terrified of what my father will say or do.

The closet door opens, my father takes a step back, glares at me, a bent paperclip in his hand. "You need to get your ass downstairs. I refuse to show up at Thanksgiving without my daughter. This is not optional."

My head is ready to explode. I stand up and pull one of my black short dresses off the hanger and then stomp over to my dresser and pull a pair of leggings out of my drawer.

My father's eyes follow me. "Do you think you could wear something other than black? Something you didn't make yourself? Do you own anything without colored stitching all over it? When are you going to wear normal clothes?" He points at me, his eyes are all glassy.

I can't believe how clueless he is. I wave my leggings in the air like a surrender flag. "Maybe if you paid any attention to me, you'd know I've been altering my clothes since seventh grade. And I'm wearing black all the time because I want to." Clutching my dress and leggings, I stomp into the bathroom and slam the door so hard the walls rattle. I wash my face and brush my teeth harder than I should, then turn the water on full blast. As I pull my shirt over my head, I pray to God and Francesca to help me get through these next hours of my life.

***

None of us says a word on the way to Grandma's house until we pull onto Grandma's street.

"You need to fix your hair, Carmella," my father says.

"I did."

"No you didn't."

"I'm wearing my hair down today and I didn't bring anything to pull it back." I figured my father would be irritated with my hair. He's never told Francesca or me why he didn't like us to wear our hair long and straight, he's only made remarks and criticisms. Francesca wore her hair down, but I've always pulled mine back in ponytails or up in a bun on holidays.

My father pulls into the driveway. He turns around.

"What the hell has gotten into you?" His face looks like old crumpled up newspaper.

"Nothing."

"Nothing? First you lock yourself in your room and then you show up at a family holiday looking like that?"

"Joe," my mother scolds.

"What? Look at her. She never wears her hair down, especially to a family holiday."

"You're getting crazy, you know that?"

My father turns back around and shuts the car off.

Mom massages her forehead. "Please, can we just go in the house and act like we're okay? The last thing I want is for everyone to worry or think the three of us can't handle our life."

"No one is going to think anything. We're going to walk in, with smiles on our faces," Dad says.

***

Mom rings the bell. I can smell the turkey out here on Grandma's porch. I wrap my hands around the sweet potato casserole a little tighter. Dad's got the cheesecake no one's going to eat and Mom's holding a small grey cardboard box. I have no idea what's inside.

Grandma opens the door, and as soon as we get in, she squeezes my cheeks and gives me a hug.

"Sweetheart." Her tone says you-poor-thing-Francesca's-gone-and-now-you're-all-alone.

Dad holds his hand out, a hanger in his other hand for our coats. Grandma gives him a hug and whispers something in his ear.

"I love your hair," Grandma says, as she strokes the back of my head while we walk into the kitchen where Aunt Maria is.

I wonder if she or anyone else is going to notice the pudge I put on over the last month.

Aunt Maria takes the lasagna out of the oven and sets it on top of the stove, turns to my dad and gives him a quick hug. "Go down to the bar and get a drink. Geo and Tony are down there. Sorry to rush you, but you're a little late."

"Could you get me a red wine, Joe?" Mom asks. "I'll help Maria."

I stand in the middle of Grandma's kitchen, feeling like a freak show. Grandma's busy making gravy, Mom's in the dining room gathering the plates for the lasagna and Aunt Maria's tossing a salad.

"Can I help with anything?" I ask.

"Honey, we're fine. You can go down with the guys," Aunt Maria says. "Tony's down there."

The door to the basement flies open. Tony's got a glass of red wine in his hand. "Uncle Joe says this is for you." He hands the wine to Mom. She sets the plates from the dining room down next to the stove and takes a sip.

"Thanks, Tony," Mom gives him a hug. "You're such a handsome boy. How's football?" she asks.

Tony puts his hands on his hips. "Football was awesome. Season's over."

"Mello, how's school?" he asks. Tony is a year ahead of me. He's a senior at St. Peter's, our so-called rivals.

"Fine," I say.

Tony walks up to me. "You should come visit me next year at Loyola. They have an awesome business program."

"I don't think I'm going into business," I say.

"That's not what your dad said in the basement," he says.

"She's undecided right now. But she's seriously thinking about a degree in business, right?" Mom says.

I look around the room full of strangers that have no idea who I am.

"I'm not thinking about majoring in business," I say.

"Carmella, don't be ridiculous. She's joking," Mom says to everyone in the room.

"You've been at Perfection since October and work so hard, you must be interested in some aspect of business," Aunt Maria says.

Aunt Maria works at Perfection in the accounting department, which is where they put me. I hate it. I hate every minute of it. Three hours, three times a week is torture.

Mom's eyes plead with me to be the daughter she wants me to be. Since Francesca's gone, I'm next in line, according to Grandpa's will. Dad's the oldest, and the son, so he gets to decide who takes over the business after him.

"The gravy is done, so let's get dinner on the table," Grandma announces. "Tony, go tell the guys."

"Carmella, honey, go sit," Aunt Maria says.

"Yeah, go ahead," Grandma says.

"But don't you need help?" I ask.

"We have everything under control," Mom says.

I walk into the dining room and find my place card decorated with a turkey, and sit. Grandma's got her good white tablecloth out, with yellow and orange napkins all around and a big paper turkey stands in the middle of the table, the kind the teachers use in the classroom when you're in second grade.

Tony, Uncle Geo and Dad come up from the basement laughing and joking around. They stop in the kitchen. Mom and Aunt Maria talk about work stuff while they dish out lasagna. Mom pops into the dining room with plates in both hands, and puts them down across the table. I stare down at my empty place, and around the empty room.

After a few minutes, everyone comes in and sits. Dad tells Tony to say the prayer. He says the normal blessing, and then he adds, "God keep our family safe that's with you now, like Grandpa and Francesca, Amen."

Mom clears her throat. "I'd like to add something." Her eyes get glassy. "Father Carlucci gave me these candles to put in the middle of the table. He says to use them as a reminder of Francesca and Frank, so their light stays with us during the ..." Mom puts her napkin up to her face, pushes away from the table and runs up the steps to Grandma's bathroom.

I push my chair out and go after her, Grandma and Aunt Maria's voices saying her name, Dad tells them I'll handle it.

I knock on the door. "Mom? You okay?"

"I'm fine, go eat. I just need a minute. Don't worry about me," she says through the closed door.

"I don't want to eat. I don't want to go back down. I want to go home."

Mom swings the door open and takes a deep breath. "We're not going home. We'll be fine. Let's not make a scene. C'mon." Mom takes me by the shoulder.

We get to the top of the steps, I stop and turn towards her. "We should have done what you wanted to do. The three of us should be doing something different this year."

"Carmella, please quit dwelling on that."

"We're never going to get over this."

"Yes we are. We need time, that's what Father says. We need to heal, that's all."

As we walk down the steps and back to the table, I feel like I'm on the sinking Titanic, but my parents don't realize the boat's sinking, so they're going along as usual, playing shuffleboard, as though water isn't gushing onto the deck.

She sits back down. "Sorry," she says. She takes a sip of wine.

"Don't apologize. We're family," Grandma says. "Losing our Francesca is tragic and we all miss Frank very much. At least we know they're both in God's hands now and someday we'll all be together."

Hearing Grandma and Father Carlucci say things like that might be comforting and make other people feel better, but not me. It's just not enough.

Chapter 10

Why I'm going to a grief support meeting

1. I'm desperate.
2. I have nothing to lose.
3. I'm sick of being afraid of my life.

December

I pull my wool hood over my head to shield my face from the wind. The winter air stings my cheeks as I walk towards downtown. It's Christmas Eve and I decided last night to take Donny's advice and go to a grief support meeting. I've been thinking about going since Thanksgiving. Mom and Dad would never understand, and since the meeting is at one o'clock today, they'll never find out. Christmas Eve landed on a Saturday, which is when this group normally meets. Mom and Dad closed the office today but they went into work to get stuff done when no one's around. They won't be home until at least three thirty.

I'm a total bag of nerves. I've never done anything like this before, but I'm desperate for help, not knowing how I'm going to survive another holiday without Francesca.

The meeting is at the Lutheran Church. I pull the stained glass door open and right away a handmade sign greets me. Green bubble letters on a piece of white paper taped to a music stand say, *Teen Grief Support Group*. A giant arrow points me in the right direction.

I walk down the hall. The same exact sign hangs on an open door of a classroom. As soon as my feet touch the doorway, a girl with red frizzy hair and freckles walks up to me. Her corduroys rub together as she moves. "Hi. You here for the support group?"

"Yeah."

"Super. Welcome. Take a seat anywhere."

The room is decorated with preschool letters and numbers in primary colors. Gold cardboard stars hang from the ceiling with kids' names on them. Tiny grey plastic chairs are set up in a circle in the middle of the room. Only two other kids are here.

I choose the chair on the side of the circle closest to the door. The two other kids are on opposite sides of me. The girl on the right has really short dark hair. Her haircut is totally cool. She's got small silver hoop earrings on and she's wearing black boots. She catches me staring at her, so I smile and look at the carpet, then unbutton my coat.

The red haired freckled girl sits down in front of us. The boy to the left of me has a navy blue down jacket on, with a matching hoody underneath. His hood is over his head. He's sort of slumped in the chair. I check out the back of the room. I wonder if someone came with him because he doesn't seem so thrilled to be here.

"Okay, let's get started. Don't use your real name unless you want to, and we never say last names. We start by everyone introducing themselves and telling us why you're here. Mrs. Silbur is running late, she's the social worker who usually runs the meeting. She got caught in traffic, so I'll start. I'm Bridget and I lost my brother three years ago to cancer." She turns to the guy with the sweatshirt.

"I'm Brian. My sister died in a car accident."

His voice is higher than I imagined. His face is completely hidden.

My turn. I'm not using my real name. "I'm Stephanie and I lost my sister at the beginning of September. She died the Saturday after school started."

I turn to awesome haircut girl.

"I'm Mattie and I also lost my sister in an accident about a year ago."

"Thanks everyone." Bridget checks her phone. "Okay, um, well, I've been coming here almost every week for about two years. It took me a year to figure out I needed to go somewhere and talk to other people dealing with the same thing as me. Anyone want to share with the group?" She smiles real big at us.

She's been coming here for like two years? Ugh. I feel worse than I did an hour ago. Everyone in this room might be dealing with death like I am, but they are light years away from understanding my crap. They aren't dealing with the same stuff I am. They didn't have a chance to prevent their sister's death, like I did. They didn't ignore their sister's call for help. If only I had put my stupid pride aside and ran over to her apartment and done what she asked me to do, she'd still be alive. I'm sure these three sitting here don't have these kinds of thoughts rolling around their brain twenty-four-seven, like I do.

My hands shake. I wonder if I should make up some story about having to go to the bathroom, but then I wouldn't be able to put my coat on. Screw it. I'm outta here. Donny's nuts.

I put my arms in my sleeves. "I gotta go."

"Oh, but I swear, Mrs. Silbur will be here in a minute. She's really helpful and will get everyone talking." Bridget stands up, her brown faded corduroys crinkled up at the knees.

"How'd your sister die?" Mattie asks without looking at me.

"An accident," I say as I pull my coat on.

"You talk about it?" Bridget asks.

"With who?" I ask.

"Anyone," Brian says.

He turns towards me and I see half of his face. He's much younger than me.

Listen to the three of them. Talk about it. Sure, I try and talk to Mom and Dad, but they don't hear me. Father Charlie helped a little bit and I talked to Donny.

"Sort of," I say.

Mattie picks at her thumb. "I feel like I have to be the glue now, to keep my parents from cracking up. It's so much pressure. And it's lonely being like an only child."

A shiver runs up my spine. The silence in this room is the kind of quiet that's dark and grey, a black kind that makes you feel like the end of the world is sitting right outside your door.

"Thanks for sharing, Mattie. Anyone else?" Bridget sits on the edge of her chair, her hands clasped in front of her.

The room suffocates me. I want to shout yes, we all lost our siblings but I'm still worse off than you are. You weren't the one who stood by the edge of the pool and watched your sister slowly drown. I can't breathe.

"Sorry." I knock over one of the mini chairs next to me. I stand it back upright. "I gotta go." I sprint to the door.

Walking through the church parking lot, I tie the belt tight around my waist and pull my hood up over my head. Stupid Donny. I spent all afternoon going over and over in my head what I would say. I was going to use my real name. I practiced how I was going to say that I lost my sister, she died of an overdose and no one seems to understand how shitty I feel.

I don't want to go home so I keep walking. I walk through the park and back around the square. The lights of the bakery are still on. I know Mrs. Sparacini's working. Christmas Eve is one of the busiest days of the year for her. I miss her and the bakery. I think I'll stop in and wish her a Merry Christmas.

***

I swing the door to the bakery open and before I'm through the door, Mrs. Sparacini's sister-in-law Lucinda screams.

"Carmella." Lucinda runs up to me and hugs me.

Mrs. Sparacini rushes over. "How are you? Merry Christmas. We miss you." She hugs me too.

She smashes my cheeks in her hands. "Oh, you're so cold, like ice. Come, sit. Lucinda will get you a hot cocoa." Mrs. Sparacini guides me over to one of the four tiny café tables. We sit down at Giovanni and Rocco's usual spot.

She holds my hand tight. "Tell me, how is everything? So hard the holidays, huh?"

I nod.

She doesn't let go. "You'll get through these tough times. Don't you ever give up. So you coming back to work?"

I'd love to say yes, I'm coming back, that's why I'm here. But I don't. I shake my head. "I can't, yet."

"I understand. Your parents, are they okay?"

I nod. "They're having a hard time I guess."

What I want to tell Mrs. Sparacini is my parents don't even talk to each other any more and when they do they end up fighting. I think they hate each other.

The bell on the door of the bakery rings. *OMG*. It's Howie.

He smiles and waves at me, I wave back.

Mrs. Sparacini pops up off her chair. She walks over to Howie, takes him by the shoulder and directs him towards me. "Two hot cocoas," she shouts.

Howie sits down.

I hope I don't fall off my chair.

"Hi." Howie takes his hat off.

"Hi," I say, feeling like someone flipped a switch. Like the whole earth just lit up and all the thunderstorms stopped. All the wars, all the fighting, and all the hate in the world just disappeared.

"So I hope I didn't interrupt some work meeting or anything," Howie says.

I want to tell him *no, you didn't interrupt anything. I stopped here after going to a meeting to try and figure out how to get my heart from bleeding on a daily basis.*

I take my coat off. I'm glad my milkshake pudge is gone. "Oh, um, I was off today and wanted to stop in and say hi." I open my eyes a little wider.

"So how was your Thanksgiving?" Howie asks.

"Okay."

"Awesome. You're lucky."

"Why?"

Howie pushes his hands in his pockets. "All holidays suck for our family, but that's the way our life is now."

"I lied. My Thanksgiving sucked too," I say with a smile I can't seem to keep off my face.

"You're lying." Howie smiles back at me.

"No, I'm not, I'm totally serious."

"Like your Thanksgiving sucked because that boyfriend of yours turned out to be a total loser, I bet."

I look down at my boots. "Not exactly."

Howie snaps his fingers. "Shoot."

I'm about to keep going with the lie.

Lucinda calls out the hot chocolate is ready. Howie and I stand up.

"No sit. I can handle a few cups," he says.

I sit back down while Howie walks over to Lucinda and gets the two cups of hot chocolate with whipped cream on top from her. Sitting here at Giovanni and Rocco's table, I think about Francesca and the worst part about losing her is up until the last month of her life, she was always there for me. Always wanted to listen to me. And now she's gone and I'm shouting on top of rooftops but nobody hears me.

Howie sets our cups down on the table. "Shucks, I'm a little disappointed your boyfriend didn't turn out to be a loser."

He was honest with me about his Thanksgiving, so I think I'll drop the boyfriend thing. "We stopped dating right before Thanksgiving. My holiday sucked because of family stuff." My hands start to sweat.

"Oh, well, so you break up with the loser and have a sucky holiday? You should have texted me. We could have wallowed in our misery together," Howie says with his arms stretched out.

"Oh," I say. I can't imagine misery happening to someone who drives a red BMW and lives where he does. People in beautiful mansions don't live in misery.

"So I know a cure for getting over bummer holiday crap real quick," Howie leans across the table.

He's totally flirting with me.

"You do?" I flirt back. He's definitely cuter since I saw him in October.

"You should come to the rink with me and skate."

"Me, ice skate? No way. I can't skate." I wave my hands in the air.

"What do you mean? Everyone can skate. Learning to skate is all about the teacher."

"No, I'm totally, completely, uncoordinated." I shake my head.

"Don't believe you."

"Cross my heart."

"I bet I can teach you."

"I bet you can't."

"What do you want to bet?"

"I don't know."

"Got plans a week from today? Saturday night?"

He totally caught me off guard. A week from today would be New Year's Eve. Gulp. Triple OMG.

"Um, you mean New Year's Eve?" I squint.

He nods and shrugs his shoulders. "You never heard of it or what?"

He's acting like it's no big deal he just asked me out on a date for the biggest night of the year. "I have another family thing. It's a New Year's Eve tradition. Been doing it since we were kids," I lie.

"No way."

"Well, yeah."

"Can you get out of your family thing? There's a fundraiser at the rink. You should come with me. I'll teach you to skate. It's for a really good cause. Give back, learn to skate, and ring in the new year all at once."

I tilt my head and smile at Howie. "You really think you can teach me to skate, don't you?"

"Yep. Like I said, let's make a bet." Howie holds his hand out.

"Okay, what do you want to bet?"

"If I *can't* teach you to go around the rink, by yourself, without falling, I will give you twenty bucks."

"Okay." I want to put my hand on the table, but can't find the guts.

"And if I *do* teach you to skate, you have to kiss me."

"What?"

Howie laughs. "Your face just turned a color not found in nature. Are you breathing?"

I throw my hands over my face, then flop them in my lap. "How do you know I won't fake it and pretend to fall, to get out of kissing you?" I laugh.

"You wouldn't."

"Why wouldn't I?"

"First of all, I'm a skater. I'd know a fake fall. Second, I think you're the honest type. And aren't you Christians supposed to go to hell for lying or something like that?"

"Got me all figured out, huh?"

"Kinda. I'll pick you up at five next Saturday."

I imagine my parents' faces. They'll freak if they think I'm going on a date, with a real guy, on New Year's Eve, so I think fast. "You're kinda pushy, you know?"

"I'll take that as a yes." Howie smiles.

"I have to work Saturday, so pick me up here."

"Totally awesome."

Howie and I talk while we finish our hot chocolate. I notice Lucinda bustling around, doing the closing routine. I check the time, and realize Mom and Dad will be home in a few minutes. I tell Howie I have to run, that I'm late for some holiday thing. I help him pick out a few pastries for his coach, who hasn't had real Italian pastries since he was in Italy. He's going to take them to the rink tomorrow morning when he practices at five a.m.

Chapter 11

Why I want to spend Christmas in my closet

1. I won't have to pretend to be happy.
2. I don't have to talk.
3. When I'm in my closet I don't hurt as much.
4. I miss Francesca.

My phone *bings*. I roll over and read the red numbers on my clock. Twelve zero zero. I don't want to get out of bed. I want to sleep all day and wake up tomorrow when the holiday is all over. I reach for my phone on my nightstand and wonder if Howie texted me.

merry christmas to all love anna

I sit up. Anna texts everyone in her phone every holiday. I want to text her back, I wonder how she is, I miss her. This is the longest we've ever gone without being in touch since we met in first grade. Even when Francesca was down and depressed and I was hanging out with her constantly, I still texted Anna. We still kept in touch. Since our big fight I've been totally avoiding her at school and lately I've been wishing we could be friends again.

I hug my knees and throw my phone down on my bed and look at Francesca's empty side of the room, remembering when she and I would wake up together on Christmas mornings. I was always up first, she always wanted to sleep longer. So I'd sit on her bed and not make a sound. She'd open one eye and roll over, trying to ignore me. When she couldn't stand it any longer she'd give in and get up so we could go downstairs and start opening gifts.

Mom's in the kitchen, making stuff for Christmas dinner. Aunt Maria offered to have Christmas, but Mom refused. She insists on trying to keep things the same. This year is our turn so we're hosting the holiday as usual.

Mom, Dad, Francesca and I used to go to church on Christmas Eve so we could sleep in on Christmas morning and open our gifts before getting together with the rest of the family. Last year Francesca skipped Christmas, and hung out with Donny instead. Christmas day was strange-weird without her, but the three of us went ahead and opened gifts as usual. We didn't even discuss the fact she wasn't with us. I'm sure we'll do the same thing today. We'll sit and open gifts and act like our family of four isn't permanently a family of three now. Last night I was thinking we should start a new tradition, like open our gifts on Christmas Eve.

***

I drag myself down the steps after showering and getting dressed. When I walk into the kitchen, Dad's getting holiday glasses down from the cabinet above the stove and putting snacks out for the family. My mother's hair is pulled back in her usual green and red Christmas barrett. She stirs the sauce for the ravioli.

"We're going to get set up for everyone, then open gifts, is that okay with you?" she asks.

"Yeah, I guess. I was thinking next year we should do something different, like open our gifts on Christmas Eve," I say.

My father closes the cabinet door. He hands me a jar of Italian dried olives from the fridge. "I don't think so."

"Why do you want to change all of our traditions, Carmella? Are we going to have to discuss this every holiday?" Mom puts her spoon down and covers the sauce.

I dig olives out of the jar. They tumble into the fake crystal bowl.

"Keeping everything the same when she's not here is wrong."

"I don't want to change what we do." My mom walks over to me.

"Can we stop beating a dead horse, please?" Dad rips open a bag of pretzel nuggets, grandpa's favorite snack.

My mother's arms twist tight around her. "Why is this so hard?" She steps towards my dad.

"Why is what so hard?" Dad pours the pretzel nuggets into a wooden bowl.

I grab the back of the chair.

"Why can't you talk about her," Mom says.

"I talk about her." He squints.

"No you don't. The only time you say something is when you want to argue with me or blame me for her problems. I think we should go talk to Father together."

"She didn't have problems. She was my daughter and I loved her. I don't need to talk to anyone. Why can't you understand I don't need to talk?" My father slams the cabinet door closed.

"Why can't we be normal again?" I look at Mom, then at Dad, hoping to get rid of the tension in the room.

"What do you mean?" Mom huffs.

"Like, try and be how we used to be when I was little," I say. "It was better then."

"You were different. You were easier, she was easier," Mom says.

"Carmella, you have to understand, things change," Dad says.

"So why do we keep doing the same things as a family?"

"We keep traditions alive. It's how we live our life," Dad says as he walks out into the living room.

I'm sick of our traditions. Our traditions aren't the same without Francesca. Nothing's the same without her. Why don't they understand?

"We need to do gifts now. They'll be here in an hour," Mom says as she sets the spoon down. Then she wipes her eyes with a paper towel and walks out of the kitchen.

***

Grandma and Mom are cutting dessert. I'm at the sink doing dishes. Tony walks in.

"Hey," I say.

Tony, Francesca and I used to hang out together at family parties and holidays when we were little. Then Francesca got to be eleven and we were too babyish for her so she'd go off on her own and Tony and I would play. But then Francesca went to college, and things changed. The three of us started hanging out again.

Tony grabs a glass from the kitchen table and plunks a few ice cubes and some root beer into it.

I turn around while I scrub a pan. "So you're totally set on Loyola then?"

"Yeah. Always had plans to go there. You know, my dad went there and everything." Tony sets his glass down and picks up a dishtowel. "Seriously, if you need to get away you can come and visit me."

I hand him the pan. "Thanks for the offer to visit, and for drying this big pan."

Tony's acting weird, like he's scared of me or I have some disease.

He gets closer. "My parents said not to say anything, but are you okay? I mean, this totally sucks. You must feel like shit, trying to celebrate a holiday and act like nothing happened."

I clear the rock out of my throat. "Yeah."

"She was a good person, a good cousin. We had a lot of fun. I miss her."

I smile. "My favorite memory was the first Christmas the three of us got to sit in the kitchen. We were so excited to be away from the adults, remember? And we were making fun of that actress, what's her name, from that movie *Enchanted* and Francesca could do the impression of her spot on." I smile.

"Oh my God, I remember. She was so good at doing impressions. And then we kept going after dinner, down in the basement," he says.

"Yeah, we got DVDs out. Francesca was so funny trying to teach us how to mimic people." I laugh.

Tony puts the pan down. We're both laughing so hard, tears fall out of my eyes. Some of them sad, some of them happy. It feels good to remember Francesca, even though it hurts like hell at the same time.

Mom walks in holding the empty creamer. She raises her eyebrow.

Tony and I stop laughing. He picks up his glass and goes back into the dining room. I turn around and finish washing the dishes.

***

I plop down on my chair behind the desk. My lunch break is over, only four more hours to go. The day after Christmas, most offices are closed, but not us. A lot of the people took a vacation day because they had to travel, so the office has a quiet, slower buzz than normal. I'm exhausted from punching numbers into a spreadsheet since eight thirty this morning.

My desk is right outside Aunt Maria's office. She does all the accounting/bookkeeping stuff and does a lot of work from home. Aunt Maria took today off, but Yolanda and I are here. Yolanda is the other half of the department. My job is to do all the idiot work for the two of them, mostly entering numbers into the computer. Mom is on the other side of the office. She handles all of the finance stuff, along with her assistant, Lisa. Mom's office is right next to Dad's.

While I punch in column after column, double-checking and triple checking my work, I think about seeing Mrs. Sparacini Saturday and being in the bakery. I totally want to quit Perfection. One last column to do for this project and I'll be done. I enter in the final number and—bam. My screen goes black.

I wonder if Yolanda's in her office. She's not, which means she went to lunch. So I walk towards Mom's office. She isn't there. She must be running an errand or something.

Dad's got Michael in his office with him. Michael is a graphic artist who has his own business. He does all the creative stuff for Perfection. Usually I would never interrupt, but this is a total emergency.

I knock on the wooden doorframe. "Sorry," I say.

Dad leans way back in his chair, his pen in his hand. "What's up?" He smiles at me.

"Hi," I say to Michael.

"How are you, Carmella?" Michael asks in the sorry-you-lost-your-sister mode.

"Okay," I say. "I have sort of an emergency and Yolanda's at lunch. My screen went black. I was almost finished with a spreadsheet. I'm worried that—"

Dad picks up his phone. "Don't panic. I'll call Ethan."

Dad gets in touch with Ethan right away. One thing about Dad is he knows how to run this business. His customers love him. He jumps right in after a huge disaster and helps them get back on their feet. People who work for him respect and like him a lot too. He's like a total hero in the disaster relief and recovery industry.

He tells Ethan my computer crashed. Watching Dad work, he's like a different person, like he time travels backwards. He's my old dad, the one who existed a few years ago. When Grandpa died and Francesca finished college something snapped inside of him.

As I turn to go back to work, I notice Michael's mock up on Dad's desk. It's pretty cool.

"Hey, you doing a new graphic?" I ask.

"Yep, Perfection needs an update. Website needs a revamp too. I'm working on a whole bunch of new stuff. Wanna check it out?" Michael turns his laptop towards me and flashes through some of his design ideas.

"I like this one," I say.

He flips to another one.

"This is cool." I smile. "Don't know if this thing works so well."

"Exactly what I was saying to your dad. You have a good eye and you're young so you're in tune with trends," Michael says. "I had no idea you were interested in this type of thing. Your dad always boasts about how good you are with numbers."

Oh my God, I want to scream how much I hate numbers, and how long it takes me to go over and over them because I make so many mistakes.

Dad hangs up. "Ethan will be over at your desk in a minute. You might need to redo the whole thing."

"You didn't tell me you were going to change all this," I say to Dad.

"Michael says we need to keep our image fresh. Image is everything," he says.

"Maybe I could help?" I ask.

Michael nods, and then scratches his shaved head. "You know—"

Dad sits up. "Carmella's got enough on her plate right now, this would be too much for her. I don't want to complicate things."

"I could do this stuff instead of accounting," I say.

Working on this kind of project would be like a dream come true for me, even better than working at the bakery.

Dad smiles. "That isn't going to teach you about how to run a business, Carmella."

He knocked the wind out of me. What, I'm here to learn the numbers? The part I hate? He's clueless as to who I am and refuses to see what I like. It's all about what he wants me to do.

I nod and make sure I smile real big, like everything is so solid with us, with our family. "Okay, no biggie. Just thought I'd ask."

As I spin around and walk back to my desk, I wonder if Dad will be proud of the perfect daughter act I just put on, exactly what I seem to do best.

I walk back to my desk and Ethan's already in my chair. He's got his chin in his hand and he's tapping on the keyboard, staring at the screen. My stomach hurts so I go to the break room and get a ginger ale. He's still pinging away when I get back.

He glances at me. "Sorry."

"Did I lose it all?"

"I think so. At least the computer is up and running. Good news is the problem was only with that one project. I'll give Yolanda and Maria a heads up." He gets up with his little handheld device and walks away.

I lost all the crap I've been working on for the last week and a half. I want to throw the computer against the wall and scream. I look towards the other side of the office. Mom's back in her chair working, Michael's in Dad's office, and they're laughing about something.

My stomach hurts so bad, I almost fall over. I walk into Mom's office. "Can I go home? My stomach hurts like heck."

Mom pops up and puts her hand on my forehead. "No fever, but you are pasty white, like you've got the flu. You better go home. You need to do anything first?"

I shake my head. "No, but I lost everything I was doing for the last week and a half. Tell Yolanda I'll start redoing it all tomorrow."

"Where is Yolanda?"

"At lunch or something." I grab my side.

***

Mom made me eat some chicken soup for dinner. I napped all afternoon, after taking three stomach pills with some ginger ale. It's eight o'clock, the TV's blasting through the wall from Mom's room. She's probably watching Lifetime. Her favorite movies are the ones where women murder their husbands.

Three quick knocks hit my door.

"Yeah?" I sit up.

My mother stands there with one hand on the knob.

"I was checking to see how you're feeling."

"I'm okay now."

Mom takes two steps forward. "Carmella. I understand you were uncomfortable this afternoon, but you seemed fine when I got home and your color is back now. What's wrong?"

"The stupid computer lost all my work and I was pissed. Then I got super bad stomach pains, I don't know why. I think something didn't agree with me from lunch."

"Yolanda had to spend the rest of her day doing your work and now has to finish the project. I was embarrassed. You should have reentered that data instead of her."

"I told you, I would work on it tomorrow. I had to leave. I couldn't work with a knife stabbing me in the gut."

My mother rolls her eyes and takes a deep breath. "Well this isn't the only thing. Aunt Maria caught a bunch of mistakes on a lot of the numbers you entered last week. You can't make mistakes, Carmella. Every number in accounting is critical. I'm surprised you're being so careless. Tony works for Aunt Maria over the summer and he's never made a mistake. Tomorrow we're going to put you with Jennifer in Sales."

"What? You don't believe me about my stomach, do you?"

"Carmella. I don't think you're sick."

"So you think I'm faking?"

"Well, you're obviously fine now. I'm not sure what to think."

"I don't care. I'm not working with Jennifer, calling people and trying to sell Perfection all day."

"She takes care of customer issues too."

"You mean customers who are pissed off and want to yell at someone."

"Carmella, watch your mouth. You'll see what your new job is tomorrow."

"No I won't."

"What do you mean?"

"I quit."

"What?"

"I quit. I'm not working for Perfection anymore. I've been thinking about quitting for a while."

"What are you talking about? You can't. We all agreed this is the best thing for you."

She means this is the best thing for her and Dad. They need to keep an eye on me, like a suicide watch. I was so disappointed when Dad wouldn't even discuss letting me work with Michael on something. I can't take another second in that office.

"I want go back to work for Mrs. Sparacini."

"You can't do that."

"Mrs. Sparacini said I could come back whenever I want to."

"But you made a commitment. We juggled responsibilities around so you'd have a job. You embarrassed us by leaving early today and made some pretty careless mistakes. And now you're going to quit?"

"I never wanted to work there. You and Dad made me."

"You know, other high school kids would love a part-time job in a family business and make the kind of money you do."

"I don't care."

"You don't care about our business? And you'd rather make half as much money at the bakery?" The veins in Mom's neck bulge.

"Yeah."

"Carmella. You can't do this. Your father is going to have a fit. We just spent an hour this afternoon with Jennifer organizing things for you. You have to stick it out."

"No."

"Why didn't you say something? Why don't you talk to me once in a while so I know what you're thinking?" Mom points her finger at me.

"I try. You don't listen."

"You should be grateful your grandfather built such a successful business. Your father's going to blow a gasket. Please stick it out." Her arms stiffen.

"Why should I?"

She steps closer to me. "Because we planned for at least one of you to take over someday. It's important to him."

Now that Francesca's gone I guess I don't have a say in the rest of my life. It used to be I was completely on my own, the invisible, silent daughter. Now I'm the pick up-the-pieces, do-what-the-first-one-didn't-do-daughter? No way.

"No." I get up. My stomach is burning, and I imagine a knife cutting me in half. I need some ginger ale. I walk past my mother, down the steps and into the kitchen. My parents have no idea that I've been living on ginger ale and pretzels for the past few weeks. During holiday meals, I'd push food around on my plate, and eat mostly plain bread. Pretzels are the only thing that doesn't make me double over in pain when I eat, which is probably why my stomach hurt after eating leftover pasta for lunch.

My dad walks in the door. Out of the corner of my eye, I watch him put his bag into the office and hang up his coat without saying a word to me. The fizz from the ginger ale bubbles up to the top of the glass. I put my hand over the rim, so I can feel the tickle on my palm. It reminds me of when my mother used to make Francesca and me ice cream floats in the summer. When we were an ice cream float kind of family—before Francesca went to college and Grandpa died.

Dad takes a beer out of the fridge, puts leftovers in the microwave and goes to get his laptop out from the office, setting it down onto the kitchen table then taking a seat in front of it. He clocks more time on his computer these days than he does talking to Mom or me. Maybe my mother's right. He's been stressed out for a long time and needs to know one of his daughters will take over for him.

I walk behind him, curious what he's working on so late. He's looking at sample websites from Michael. That ticks me off.

"I'm quitting."

My dad keeps tapping at the keyboard.

"Did you hear me? I quit."

The microwave stops and the bell rings.

My dad gets up and walks over and opens the microwave. "Shouldn't you be in bed? I thought you were sick."

"Did you hear me?"

"No, what." Dad blinks.

"I quit. I'm not working for you anymore." I squeeze my hands together, terrified he's going to blow up.

"What? Yes you are."

"No, I'm not."

"Where the hell do you come off thinking you can quit? I had Jennifer spend the afternoon creating another job for you in the sales department because you screwed up the first one."

"You created a job for me because you decided I need to work at Perfection. And then you don't let me do an interesting job. You give me a stupid numbers job."

"That stupid numbers job is so you'll learn the business, see the inside of what we do. It's the best way to learn what's going on."

"Says who?"

"Says me."

"I don't care. I want to go back to the bakery."

"You do not want to go back to the bakery. You just want to be a rebel like your sister."

"I want to do something I want to do, not enter data into a computer all afternoon like a stupid idiot or listen to people bitch about your company's mistakes."

"For your information, our mistakes are few and far between. And second, you are learning a family business. Something you used to say you were interested in before you started that asinine bakery job."

"I was never interested in Perfection."

"Not interested? You seem to be interested in reaping the benefits of having a nice car, a nice house, and going to a private school."

"I hate the school, I hate this house and you don't let me drive anymore."

"You'd rather go work for a stranger than work for us?"

"Yeah. I hate working with numbers."

"You used to be so responsible. What the hell's gotten into you?"

"I checked all the numbers I input three times. I try hard not to make mistakes but sometimes I can't help it. If you'd let me work with Michael, I wouldn't make mistakes."

"So you want to quit learning about the business and focus on logos and websites?"

"Yeah."

"Well, that's not the way it works." My dad paces the kitchen like a caged lion.

I want to scream at him that he doesn't understand me at all. Why doesn't he hear me?

My mother stands in the doorway of the kitchen. "What the hell is going on down here?"

"I just told Dad."

"You know about this?" he asks.

"She just told me, Joe, let it go. I tried to talk her out of it, but she wants to go back and work at Il Milano."

"Here you go again. Giving in."

"Joe."

"I'm sick of you going against me," he says.

"I'm sick of you being stubborn." Mom balls her hands into fists.

"I thought we agreed to keep an eye on her so she doesn't make mistakes with her life like Francesca did." My father stabs his finger at my mom.

I'm suffocating like someone put a pillow over my head. "I'm going back to the bakery. You can't rule my entire life." I spin around and race up the steps.

My father shouts. "I'm taking your car to the office tomorrow. I'll sell it to James or Colin. Find your own way around from now on."

"Fine. The only reason you gave me a car is so I could go check up on Francesca," I yell from the top of the steps.

I run into my room, slam the door as hard as I can and throw myself onto the bed. I scream into my pillow. They're making my life worse. I sit up and stomp over to my guitar, grab the neck, John Lennon's character sketch staring back at me. I let go and sit down on my bed. My parents argue in the kitchen, their voices get louder. My eyes ache, my head hurts and a sharp knife stabs me in the stomach. I grab my pillow, hold it tight and lie down.

My messenger bag is still sitting on the floor in front of my closet, where it's been since winter break started. The crumpled up French brochure pokes out the side.

France. Right now I'd give anything to go to France. I roll over and stare at the ceiling. Tears fall down the side of my face and land in my ears. I imagine for a second what life would be like away from here. Away from my parents who have only two modes: Silent and Fight. I imagine myself living in Paris, with a family who would understand who I am and what I need. I slide off the bed and grab the brochure. I look for the deadline for scholarship applications. I grab a pen and fill out the application, my eyes blurry, my nose running. I'll drop it off with my guidance counselor the first day of school next week. And I'm going get my job back at the bakery tomorrow. I can't live like someone's holding my head under water all the time.

Chapter 12

Why I'm scared to take a chance with my heart

1. I might not recover.
2. Not taking any chances is easier.

New Year's Eve

Howie picks me up at five o'clock from work, like we planned. Mrs. Sparacini was thrilled when I went into the bakery four days ago to tell her I wanted to come back. Her sister in-law Lucinda was happy too. I found the guts to tell Mrs. Sparacini I needed to get out of the house the last few days of winter break so I could work every day if she needed me to. I didn't have the guts to tell her I want to learn how to decorate cakes, but I will after I get back into the swing of things.

***

As we walk into the ice rink, the smell of popcorn and hot dogs makes me think I'm at a carnival. The girl behind the long grey folding table with the cash box in front of her tells Howie she can't wait to see his new routine.

I turn to Howie. "What does that mean?"

Howie walks me over to some benches so I can sit while he laces up his skates. He twirls the numbers on his locker and sets a gym bag down on the bench. He sits next to me and pulls a skate out of the black bag.

Loosening up the laces he says, "Before the free skate, I'll be performing in an exhibition. A bunch of skaters headed for Nationals in a few months are going to do our routine tonight. You interested in watching?"

"Oh my God, how exciting. Yeah, I'm gonna watch. Unless you don't want me to. Would it be better if I stay out here?"

"No. Not at all. I'd love it if you were in the stands."

"So why didn't you tell me about this?"

"It's the way I roll. Telling you would have worked on my head too much, you know?"

"Yeah, sure." I have no idea what Howie's talking about. Sitting on my bed and singing to a pretend audience, I don't have to worry about stuff like that.

Howie walks me into the rink and introduces me to a couple of girls and guys my age who are super friendly and act like they're Howie's best friends. They tell me I can sit with them. After a few minutes the music comes on and the girl next to me, Nikki, gives me the low down of the whole event and how many skaters will be performing in the next hour.

The lights dim and the first skater is announced. I'm amazed how good she is. Two more skaters come out, doing spins and all kinds of moves like in the Olympics.

Nikki taps me on the arm and points to Howie, who's waiting at the side of the rink with his coach. Howie's dressed in total black and cracking his neck. He looks different. Taller, older, way too serious for him. Not like the usual joking-around-all-the-time Howie.

Howie skates into the middle of the rink and stops, his arms behind his back, his head down. John Lennon's "Whatever Gets You Through the Night" blares. He starts his routine and I get goose bumps all over.

Howie does his first jump. Everyone claps and whistles. As Howie skates, I forget it's him on the ice. I can't believe how good he is. The song ends, and the first notes of "Imagine" float out from the speakers. My throat closes up. I don't want to cry like a baby and I can't leave and go have a meltdown in the bathroom, so I focus on Howie.

Lucky for me, the music quickly changes and "Sgt. Pepper's Lonely Hearts Club Band" plays. Nikki nudges me. "Watch," she whispers. "He's getting ready to do a triple. He's been messing up all week at practice." I keep my eyes on him, terrified he's going to fall. Howie does the triple loop, lands a little sideways on his skate, but catches himself and doesn't fall.

Howie finishes his program, the crowd is on its feet, cheering. People behind me whistle. Howie takes a bow before he skates off the ice, looking right at me through the glass. A beam of light hits my heart.

Howie's coach is waiting for him right when he gets off the ice. He talks to him for a minute, then Howie waves to me and points to the door. I turn to Nikki, not knowing what the heck he's talking about. She says he'll meet me at the bottom of the stands after the last skater skates.

Two more skaters perform and when they're done, the rink manager comes out onto the ice to thank us all for attending this fundraiser in honor of Howie's twin brother and sister who died at two years old of Krabbe's Disease, a rare genetic disease that affects the nervous system. The words knock the wind out of me. Howie? I can't believe something this bad happened to him. I wonder where his parents are?

Howie meets me at the bottom of the stands. I reach out for his hand, and hold on tight. I want to say something to him about what I just heard but don't know if I should. He directs me through the crowd up to the skate rental counter. The girl asks me what size shoe I wear, then plunks a pair of skates down in front of me. Howie says he'll put them on for me as we walk back to the benches. I sit down while he pulls a towel out of his bag and wipes his face and neck. Other skaters walk by and high five Howie in the air while they keep talking and laughing, the sounds of their voices echoing through the rink.

I want to talk to Howie about Francesca, but at the same time I'm scared. I think he's the first person that might understand where I'm coming from. Plus, I wonder if he needs to talk to someone about his family too. But I can't. I can't even say Francesca's name out loud, so I decide to talk about skating.

"You didn't tell me you were an Olympic skater."

Howie sits down. "Not even close to Olympics anymore, but thanks." Howie grabs a blue torn up towel out of his bag and wipes the water off his blades.

I wonder if he needs to talk about the twins. "I'm sorry about your brother and sister. I had no idea the fundraiser was for them. You didn't tell me." I can't imagine how his family is surviving. It seems so horrible and unfair.

"Sorry. I guess I should have given you a heads up." Howie wipes his left blade until it shines.

"No, it's okay. Believe me, I suck at bringing up things like that." I twist my hands together. I take a deep breath. I want to talk about how much I miss my sister, I wonder why people have to die, and every day since Francesca's been gone, I wonder if God even exists. "How, I mean, when did all this happen?"

"I was in fourth grade when they died. My parents are totally messed up now, but I'm the one going to a shrink once a week. Crazy, right?"

I nod. "I totally get what you mean."

"You got parents who need a shrink but they send you to get your head shrunk instead?"

"Something like that." I take a huge breath in and jump off my cliff. "I, well, I lost someone too—my sister."

Howie stops wiping the other blade. "I'm sorry. When?"

"About four months ago."

"Accident?"

Howie takes my hand. I almost pull away but I don't. I open my mouth to blurt out the whole messed up truth of everything, right here, right now. I want to tell him. I want to finally tell somebody what goes on in my head twenty-four-seven, but he might think I'm a total-loser-crazy-person.

I hold his hand a little tighter. "Yeah." I look down at his skate. I change the subject. "You are such an awesome skater. I had no idea."

"Thanks. You need to take your shoes off," he says.

"What?"

"Skates?" He waves a skate up in the air.

"Oh, right. Sorry." I laugh. I unlace my army boots and take them off, pushing them under the bench with everyone else's shoes. I push my feet into the skates. Howie stands up, grabs my right skate and rests it on his leg. He laces up the skate, his hands moving like he's done this two million times. I bite my cheeks a little and sit on my hands. The thought of trying to stand up on these little blades is frightening. I can only imagine what's going to happen to me when we get out on the ice.

Howie raises one eyebrow. "Nervous?"

"Sorta." I roll my eyes. I'm such a baby. He's out spinning and jumping on the ice like an Olympiad and I'm terrified of standing up.

He laughs.

After he laces up the other skate, he grabs my other hand and helps me get up. My ankles wobble back and forth. I wonder if while we're skating he's going to tell me he's leaving for Russia to go train for the Olympics like tomorrow morning.

"You headed to the Olympics or what?"

Howie smiles. "I wish. Competition was fierce this year. It's probably the end for me."

How could this be the end? I thought I was the only one God dished the crap to. "You mean quit or like the end of the year-end?"

"End of skating, period. The reality of skating ten hours a day isn't practical anymore. I need to stop competing. Besides, my parents will be on top of the world when I quit and focus on medical school.

"Oh yeah, Jeremy said you wanted to be a doctor."

"He was jacking with you. That's not true."

"So what do you want to do?"

"I'm not sure but I don't want to be a doctor."

I look around and realize I haven't met Howie's parents. "By the way, where are your parents?"

"Working. They started this fundraiser, they used to come and be totally into it, but they don't anymore. They don't do a lot of things now. They're never gonna get over the twins."

A cute blonde in skates yells from across the rink, pulling her gloves over her hands. "Hey, you skating or what?"

Howie yells, "On our way." He takes a quick glance down at my feet, then into my eyes. "You ready?"

"Yeah. I think so." My ankles hurt already.

He walks me over to the doors of the rink. My ankles keep falling to the sides. I'm positive that I'm going to make an ass out of myself.

"Maybe I shouldn't skate."

"You'll do great. Trust me, the rink is the perfect place for attitude adjustments."

"So you think I need an attitude adjustment?" I put my hand on my hip, a little more at ease with him.

"Everyone needs an attitude adjustment once in a while," he says.

We walk to the edge of the rink and Howie glides onto the ice. He holds his hand out to me. My right skate touches the slippery ice and flies out from under me. I grab onto the side railing, desperate to not fall. I must look like a cat clawing its way out of a bathtub.

Howie makes a face. "You really haven't been on skates before, have you?"

"I told you. I can't do this. I'm going to sit down."

Howie grabs my hand, "Oh no you don't. I'm teasing. Everyone starts out all awkward."

"Yeah, but I think it's too late for me."

"Nope, never too late." Howie laughs.

He grabs my other hand and gently leads me onto the ice. My ankles won't cooperate, they've turned into rubber. Doing anything would be better and easier than this. Little four-year-olds twirl and spin, while Howie's stuck holding my two hands like a dad who's trying to help his wobbly baby take her first steps.

As my feet slip, he coaches me. "... push with the right, glide ... then push with the left ... slow. Easy. Push, push. Don't lift up."

He smiles. "I think you might be catching on."

I almost fall backwards. "You are sooo not funny. You're totally making fun of me."

"No I'm not. I'm serious. You should be doing way worse than you are."

"Thanks."

"Here, hold onto my waist." Howie lets go of my hands and stands with his backside in front of me.

A voice screams inside my head. *Are you kidding me? I'm supposed to hold onto your what?* I tell myself to stay cool, grab his waist and be calm. Terrified, I only use the tips of my fingers. *Why am I doing this?*

He stops, spins around, looks up at the ceiling and into my eyes. "You gotta hold on tight. This pansy-ass thing doesn't fly. You wanna learn or not?"

"No. I don't. I changed my mind. Let's go." I try and turn around but lose my balance. I forget I'm on ice.

Howie grabs my waist from behind as I start to fall. "No way." He laughs. "We're not leaving this rink until you how to skate. I don't quit and I don't like to lose—at anything."

He gently takes my hands and plants them on his sides, keeping a tight grip on them. I stare at his back.

"Urgh." I take a deep breath, mad at Howie for making me do this and totally liking it, all at the same time.

I cringe.

"Look at my feet and copy what I do. Ready?"

"Ready," I mumble.

It's hard for me to focus, to concentrate, to forget my hands are on Howie's waist. But after a few minutes, my heart stops racing and my skates glide easier. Besides, after what Howie said, I don't have a choice but to skate if I ever want to leave this ice rink. Plus, I'm not a quitter either.

We skate for almost a half hour. My shins and ankles burn. They hurt so bad I forget all about touching Howie. I'm scared to admit to him how much my legs and ankles hurt, so I stare at his butt to try and forget about the pain.

As if he's figured out what I was doing, he moves from in front of me to right next to me, and holds my hand. I'm practically skating all by myself. I'm slow, but I'm skating and I think I'm having fun. He keeps an eye on me, correcting me to not put too much pressure on one of my skates. For a few minutes, we skate, without saying a word and I forget about my life.

"Now we're gonna do something different," Howie says.

He grabs my left hand. "Don't let go of my hands. This is the part where you keep skating forward, like you're doing, and I'm gonna skate backwards. I'll pull you a little, but don't panic. Listen to the music, sing along in your head, let it guide you, and follow my lead."

My ankles and shins are burning. "Can we take a break first?"

"Not yet. After this song," he says.

The music changes. I recognize the song. "Drops of Jupiter" from the band Train echoes through the rink.

Howie counts the beats before the next verse.

I laugh, thinking for sure he's going to break out in song, but he doesn't.

Then he takes my right hand and lays it on his shoulder as though we're dancing.

"Watch. Do what I do."

My left hand is on his shoulder and my right hand's stretched out inside of his, like we're doing the waltz or something. His head is so close to mine, I try to avoid looking straight into his eyes.

I feel him breathe and smell that same woodsy smell of him, like at the night of the party. He smiles at me, and I smile back. Being with him is so easy, but so weird at the same time. He's like a new and different person, but I also feel like I've known him forever. Gliding to the music, moving together, Howie catches my eyes with his and doesn't look away. His hair sweeps across his forehead.

The song ends, the whistle blows and an announcer says break time. The Zamboni idles, waiting to barge onto the ice.

"C'mon. We got a ten minute break." Howie and I skate to the end of the rink. Right before we get to the railing, my foot slips out from under me. "Shit." My arms fly up in the air. Howie catches me and pulls me up.

"Thanks for saving me." I laugh.

"No problem. I got your back." Howie smiles. "By the way, I think you owe me."

"What?"

"The bet?"

"No way. I don't owe you. I fell."

"No. That wasn't a fall. You slipped." Howie laughs.

"If you weren't here to catch me I would have fallen."

"Exactly," he says.

Howie doesn't let go of my hand. When we get to the benches he leans in and kisses me right on the lips. I want to scream and run but the kiss was so fast my ankles turned to jelly and if Howie weren't holding my hand, I'd be on the floor right now.

***

After the fundraiser, Howie surprises me and takes me to a cute tiny French restaurant close to where he lives. A husband and wife own it. They used to live in France and they act like they know him. We're sitting at a little table in the window and I order the same thing as Howie. I'm being polite, but I also thought the Chicken Dijon sounded sort of exotic and very French.

I never had food that tasted so good in my whole life. Nina the wife comes over right after our plates are taken away. She's round, with blond frizzy hair up in a messy bun. She gently sets a mini heart-shaped chocolate cake down in the middle of the table with a red rose on top.

She clasps her hands proudly in front of her. "You two enjoy. Dessert is on the house for the most adorable young couple of the night." Her smile is as big as the state of Montana. "Happy New Year," she does a kiss in the air to us.

Howie and I laugh as we take a bite of the cake.

Howie finishes chewing. "So now that you heard all about my skating life since I was like two years old, tell me how you started writing songs." He licks his lips and leans in a little.

The taste of sweet-bitter chocolate lingers on my tongue. I take a sip of water and clear my throat. "Wow. No one's ever asked me that." I push my hair behind my ear. "One day I had words pop into my head and I sort of heard them like a song. So I started playing around with the words and music."

"A broken-hearted love song?"

"No. It was …" I smile and look out the window, totally embarrassed.

"C'mon. It wasn't about a bunny, was it?" Howie laughs.

"Noo, I'm not that dorky."

"So tell me. I'm dying to know what inspired you to write your first song," Howie smiles.

"Promise you won't laugh?" I smirk.

"Promise."

I take a deep breath. "Okay, the city."

"Like Chicago?"

"Yeah. My parents took us into the city to see our first play at the Auditorium Theatre, the summer after my eighth grade graduation. We were all walking down Michigan Avenue and all the horns blasting, the street musicians, people rushing, it was so exciting. As I took each step, I felt a beat, and I heard music in my head. The next morning I got up and the words poured out and I wrote my first song.

"So what instrument do you play?"

I can't tell him the truth. Thinking about the word guitar is starting a chain reaction in my head I don't want to deal with right now. So I think fast. "We have a piano." I change the subject. "Giving us this cake is so nice," I say. "You know them?"

"My parents used to come here a lot. Awesome place, huh?"

I nod, trying to picture Howie's parents. I wonder what they're like. "Yeah, I think this was like the best meal of my entire life." I won't tell Howie this has been the best five hours of my entire life too.

"Totally," he says. "So you sure you need to be home by ten thirty?"

"Yeah. My parents are sort of control freaks these days."

"I thought if you could stay out later, we could hit a party, since it's New Year's Eve and all. There's a couple of them going on. You and I could kick butt on the dance floor."

I don't want this night to end, but I don't want to stir up crap at home. "Maybe another time?"

***

My parents think I'm out with Anna. Halfway home, I decide I need to be super safe, so I'll tell Howie drop me off down the street from where I live. I don't want to risk Mom and Dad seeing Howie's car and freaking out about where I was and who Howie is. I don't want to end this night with a fight.

"So this is gonna sound crazy, but I need you to drop me off a block from my house."

"What? You're joking, right?"

"No."

"No way am I going to be a dick-wad and drop you off in some random place in the middle of the night."

"It's not the middle of the night, it's not random and you won't be a dick-wad."

Howie's got a totally weird expression on his face.

I'll tell him the story I came up with in my head when we passed the Walgreen's about mile ago. "My mom has the flu and she's a really light sleeper. Her, I mean, my parents' window faces the driveway. She'll hear the car and wake up and I don't want to disturb her."

"Seriously?"

"Yeah."

"Okay, so I'll park the car a block away and walk you home."

"No, no no. You don't have to do that."

"Yes I do."

"Really, you don't."

"I'm gonna anyhow."

"Howie."

"Carmella."

Howie stops the car a block away and turns the engine off.

"It's December and cold," I say.

"Exactly why you shouldn't walk alone, besides."

"Besides what?"

"Are you gonna make me say it?"

"Say what?"

"I don't want to leave you by the side of the road on our first date."

"First date?"

"Yeah, first date."

"You sure you're not a chick?"

"Okay, that's it. You're in for it." Howie pulls the keys out of the car and undoes his seatbelt. He acts like he's going to wrestle me.

"In for what?" I undo my seatbelt, open the door and run as fast as I can.

Howie catches up to me and grabs me by the waist. He starts to tickle me and I can't figure out if I'm laughing or doing my usual freak out.

Howie stops tickling me and leans in a little bit. His head is half an inch from mine. My panic mode kicks into high gear. I pull my hands away and jump back. Howie looks confused.

"Sorry." I need to make up a lie to cover up my freak out. He was about to kiss me again. "I think I pulled my leg muscle down here." I grab my calf, my purse falling off my shoulder, my jacket all twisted up. I'm such an idiot, but I can't do it. I can't let him kiss me and I have no idea why. It's terrifying.

"Here, let me see." Howie bends down to look at my leg.

"It's okay. I'll be fine."

Howie and I stand up straight. He reaches his hand out to me. "I know how it hurts."

I take Howie's hand as we walk towards my house.

"Thanks for tonight. I had fun," I say. I want to tell him I haven't laughed so much since before Francesca moved out. I want to be honest and tell him I wanted to kiss him a minute ago, but for some reason I panicked.

"I had fun too," Howie says. He gives me a dramatic once-over. "I like your coat. It's different. You're different. "

"Different. That doesn't sound good." I scrunch my nose up.

Howie laughs. "I mean different in a good way. Different like in creative, like a true artist. So what else do you do outside of school besides song writing?"

I look down at the stitching on my sleeve. I love to make everything I wear my own. I hate looking like everyone else and I love working with fabrics.

"I guess I like to alter all my clothes and make them unique. Sort of take what exists and make it better."

"Awesome. Everyone in your school dresses the same—they have to. But in my school where anybody can wear anything? All the girls wear totally the same clothes. But you're like an original. Original beauty like the kind that inspired all the famous artists."

Thank God it's dark outside because my face turned magenta.

Three more houses until I'm home.

When the two of us step onto my front lawn, I notice how dark our house is and I sort of die a little inside. "Well, here I am."

"Hey, text me. I skate tomorrow, but that's all. You busy?" Howie asks.

"Just working."

"So Happy New Year," Howie says, his breath floating towards me.

He grabs my other hand and leans in.

"Oh, you too. Totally forgot." I hug him.

I start to walk backwards, wave at him and run. "Bye. Thanks again. I'll text you." If I were a normal girl, I'd at least blow Howie a kiss. But then again, I've never felt like a normal girl.

Howie smiles, shakes his head and waves back.

When I get to the front door, I peek down the street and watch Howie walk. He turns around and I wave. He waves back. I open the front door, all light and foggy, like the world might be a little brighter.

***

I'm sitting in my closet, clutching Francesca's purse on New Year's Day. My phone has two texts from Howie on it. One telling me he had an awesome time last night and the second one asking me if I want to go over to Nikki's house for a New Year's Day bash with some of the skaters I met last night.

My finger's on the send button, but I haven't done it yet. My text says, *Thx but already have plans.* I totally want to get together with Howie, but I can't do it. I don't know why, but I can't. I press send. I throw my phone down, hug Francesca's purse a little harder, and curl up in the dark quiet closet. A few minutes later, I pick up my songpad and instead of writing a song or a list, I draw a tree with bleeding hearts hanging from its branches.

Chapter 13

Reasons why I've been turning down dates from Howie

1. I'm scared.
2. I like him too much.
3. Mom and Dad will freak out and they'll treat me like Francesca.

I open the door and pull off my hat and gloves, relieved to get out of the cold dark winter morning. Mrs. Sparacini and Lucinda are racing around, getting ready for a busy Saturday at the bakery. Since Dad took the car away, I walk everywhere, except when I'm running late for school and Mom gives me a ride. Lucky for me the bakery is only two miles away from home and school. As I head towards the back to hang up my coat, Mrs. Sparacini runs up to me and puts her hands on top of my head.

"Oh my God, when did you cut your hair? You're beautiful, but why?"

I push my bangs over to the side. "I saw this haircut on a girl way back in December. I've been thinking about a change for a while and yesterday found the guts to do it."

"Well good for you. I love it. I can really see those big beautiful brown eyes of yours. And your Howie must love it."

"He hasn't seen me yet. We haven't seen each other since our New Year's Eve date."

"You haven't seen him in two weeks?"

We both push through the door going into the back room.

I hang my coat up and put my apron on. "He asked me out a bunch of times, but I've been super busy." I tie the strings tight behind me.

Mrs. Sparacini laughs while she shoves a giant box of baking soda on the shelf. "Well, I'm sure he'll love your hair. You should show off that beautiful face." She turns around, walks over to me and squeezes my cheeks. "You better stop running."

"What?" I ask her.

"Stop running." She walks back to her office.

The bell on the front door of Il Milano rings but I don't run out to the front. Mrs. Sparacini's sister in-law Lucinda will take care of the usual Saturday morning customers. I found the nerve three days after I started working again over winter break to tell Mrs. Sparacini that I wanted to learn to decorate cakes. She screamed she was so happy. She said she wanted me to practice piping first thing when I get into work so I'm fresh and not too tired. So I pipe on a cookie sheet with leftover icing for about an hour. Mrs. Sparacini says as soon as I get good enough, she'll let me help her decorate real cakes and give me a raise, possibly in time for Valentine's Day, which is in exactly one month.

Mrs. Sparacini has no idea that teaching me how to decorate cakes has saved me from going totally insane. When I'm holding the pastry bag in my hand, I forget about how shitty my life is without Francesca and my brain gets a break from having to think about everything that bugs me, like Mom and Dad and the stress factor in our house. They barely speak to each other and Dad's moved into the guest room.

I worked every day during winter break, trying to practice a lot in case I end up going to culinary arts school in France. Plus, the more I work the more money I'll save. I pray every day that I get into the study abroad program and out of my house.

"Carmella? There's a customer who wants to speak to you," Lucinda shouts from the front.

"Be right out," I shout.

I'm thinking its Mrs. Venizio. She comes in every Saturday to pick up a dessert for her and Mr. Venizio. I wrap up her pastries and she tells me all about her kids, about how they never come home to visit her anymore. She likes me to wait on her for some odd reason.

I push the doors open. Howie's standing in front of the pastry case.

"Hi." Howie smiles at me. "Oh my God, where's all your hair?" Howie holds his hands up in the air and laughs.

My heart free-falls. "I did it yesterday." My face turns colors.

Howie smiles. "I love it." Howie stuffs his hands into the front pockets of his grey cargo shorts. He leans over the bakery case.

"Serious?" I say.

"Come here. Let me check it out," he says.

"You hate it, don't you?" I smooth the back of my head, knowing he's going to think I'm ugly.

"No, I love it. You look … more like *you*," Howie says.

"I do?" I rake my fingers through the short, messy pieces of hair.

"Yeah. What possessed you?" he asks.

"I don't know, I got tired of having to put my hair in a pony all the time and wanted a change."

Mrs. Sparacini comes up behind me and puts her hands on my shoulders. "You two should take a walk. Get some coffee or tea or whatever you young people drink these days. Be back in thirty minutes. I want you to practice piping before we get too busy."

We both look at Mrs. Sparacini.

"Go!" She shoos us like we're farm animals.

"I guess we're going for a walk," Howie says.

"But it's freezing out there."

Mrs. Sparacini hands me my coat, Lucinda crosses her arms and raises her eyebrows.

"I guess I'm going." I scrunch my nose up at Mrs. Sparacini.

Howie and I walk down Third Street towards the middle of town where the gazebo is.

Howie takes my hand and I can't believe how awesome it is to see him. I'm totally fighting off a huge smile that keeps creeping onto my face and I want to jump up and down, scream and wave my arms in the air and shout, *I like him, I like him, I like him so much.*

"Sounds like you're just learning to decorate cakes." Howie turns to me as we walk down the sidewalk. He smiles with a raised eyebrow.

He remembered my lie. "Yeeaah. Anna was just making up that whole cake decorator thing before. But now I'm official." I hold my arms out.

"How is Anna?" Howie asks.

"Good," I lie, afraid to tell Howie we still don't speak to each other.

I give Howie a dramatic up and down. "So what's up with the early morning visit?"

"I wanted to ask you something."

We cross the street.

Howie points to a coffee shop. "Want a hot chocolate?"

"Sure."

Howie swings open the door of the Elmwood coffee shop. My stomach is a little green, remembering the last time I was here with Donny, or maybe because I'm sure Howie needs to tell me I'm a nutcase and he's deleting me from his phone and his life. I wonder how Donny is.

After we get our drinks and ease into a few oversized puffy chairs in the corner, I freak out. I take a sip of the hot chocolate and burn the shit out of my tongue, yanking the cup away and spilling a few drops on my jeans like an idiot.

Howie jumps up and gets a bunch of napkins for me. "Yeah. That's why they call it *hot* chocolate."

"Thanks. For the napkins *and* smart-ass commentary."

Howie laughs. "So, are you doing anything for Valentine's Day? I mean, besides making heart-shaped cakes?"

"Um, no." I try to rub the spot away. Howie totally caught me off guard. I wonder why is he asking me out for Valentine's Day now?

"Good. You want to go to the *Rocky Horror Picture Show*? I have to order tickets now for the Friday before Valentine's Day, the tenth. My parents are going to be out super late, they've got one of their benefit dinners, so we could go hang at my place afterwards. I also wondered if you could ask Anna with an attitude if she wanted to go with Jeremy. We could do a double thing. He's been dying to call her, but keeps chickening out. I told him I'd ask you to ask her. Spare his ego, you know?"

"Oh, well, I'm sure she'd go out with him. I could ask her for you, if you want." I think about how this might be exactly what we need to get over our fight, I miss her.

"So you'll talk to her?"

"Yeah, sure."

"Does that mean you're actually saying yes to me?"

I smile wide and hold my arms out. "Yes!"

***

I walk back into Il Milano. Mrs. Sparacini and Lucinda are beaming.

"So? What happened?" Mrs. Sparacini follows me while I hang up my coat and put on my apron.

"Nothing."

"Nothing? That boy is crazy about you," Lucinda says.

My ears heat up.

"Boys don't come in and surprise girls at work this early in the morning for no reason. Did he ask you to a dance, to go steady, what?" Mrs. Sparacini asks.

"He just asked me out for Valentine's Day."

"*Just*? Asking a girl for a date a month in advance? I think he's trying to tell you something."

"Nah, it's nothing. He has to get tickets," I say.

"You both light up like Christmas trees when you're together," Mrs. Sparacini says.

She's totally rocking my world.

"I don't think so."

Mrs. Sparacini walks up to me. "What is wrong?"

I pick at my thumb. "I don't know. I might cancel. I don't think I'm ready for this big Valentine's Day thing, lots of people, crowds." As the words come out of my mouth, I realize going out with Howie on Valentine's Day means being with a person Francesca never met.

I feel like I'm planning a game of hide and seek and Francesca will never be able to find me.

Mrs. Sparacini puts hands on her hips. "I see how you look at him. I also know Francesca would want you to be happy. I don't think you should let her down."

Mrs. Sparacini's words slowly travel into a dark corner of my soul. I try to keep them from reaching a spot where they'd make a difference, but I can't.

***

When I get home, I text Anna and tell her I have to talk to her. She texts me back and says she's not speaking to me since I don't accept apologies. I text Howie and tell him she said no to Jeremy, sorry.

Chapter 14

Why I want to go to France

1. I can reboot my life.
2. I could learn about the culinary arts and the culture.
3. The art.
4. The food.
5. The Eiffel Tower.

February

"Thanks, Mrs. Farmington," I wave to my guidance counselor as I walk out of her office. I finally handed in my scholarship application for France. Today's Tuesday, February seventh, the last day to apply. I knew I'd end up in a fight with my parents over the whole idea, so I went ahead and forged their signatures. Mrs. Farmington suggested I take another brochure about financial aid, since my grades have slipped and I probably won't be eligible. I'm sure my parents would never pay for me to go, but I take the brochure from her anyhow.

I can't take my eyes off the Eiffel Tower on the cover. I want to get out of here so badly and live somewhere where people are more like me, where I belong. I wonder if God made a big mistake and put

Francesca and me with the wrong parents. We should be daughters of artists or musicians or actors, not people who run a cleaning and disaster-recovery business.

Bam. I slam into someone with my shoulder.

"Shit." I pick the brochure up from the ground. Anna is standing right in front of me.

"What the hell?" Anna pulls her bag back up onto her shoulder. "Oh my God, your hair."

"Girls." The secretary scowls at us from her desk. "Take your conversation outside please."

Anna and I make eye contact and crack up, just like we did when we had to listen to the fourth grade sex talk and we had a totally uncontrollable laughing fit. We were kicked out and sent straight to Sister Margaret's office. I wonder if Anna's thinking the same thing.

We hold our hands over our mouths and push through the double glass doors into the chattering hallway, swarms of kids everywhere.

Anna turns to me. "You okay?"

"Yeah, you?"

"You totally chopped your hair off."

"Does it look like shit? Oh my God, I look like shit, don't I?"

"No, no. You look awesome, you look sooo different," Anna says.

"I'm sorry. Do you hate me?" I ask.

"I don't hate you, do you hate me?"

"I was super mad, I'm sorry," I say.

"I'm sorry too," Anna says. "We've been friends since first grade. We're supposed to be blood sisters. Remember when we poked our fingers with a pin in second grade?"

"Yeah," I say. I do remember the afternoon, swearing to each other for forever, no matter what, we'd be friends. I'm such a loser. I totally blew her off when she reached out to me during the holidays, knowing I would hurt her. I'm a terrible friend. I know we'll never be the same. Things will never be like they were before Francesca died. I'm in a giant chalk circle on the driveway and the only way Anna will be able to come in is when she experiences the pain of losing someone like I have.

"I'm sorry. I'm a shitty friend," I say.

I want to tell her how much I miss her and want us to be friends again. I don't think I can live without her.

"Can I tell you something?" I ask.

"Yeah."

"It hurts to see you."

"What do you mean?"

"I mean, I think you remind me of my life before Francesca died."

"So you can't be friends with me?"

"Maybe I could if you cut your hair or grow a mustache."

"Whatever you need me to do, just tell me and I'll do it."

We both laugh.

"Want a ride home or to work?" Anna asks.

"No thanks. I'm kind of in the habit of walking." I remember the Valentine's double date. I'm sure Anna would want to go now and I'd love us to go together but I want to ask her when we have more than a second to talk. "But, I have so much to tell you, wanna do lunch?"

"Yeah, sure. How about Wendy's?"

Anna and I used to hit Wendy's every Friday for lunch.

"Yeah."

"Meet me at my car at eleven twenty."

"I'll be there."

On my way to science, I think about Anna and me and how weird it felt talking to her. Like we're friends who just met. I hope that strange awkwardness goes away.

***

The Wendy's is packed with people. I stare ahead at the menu and the employees in the goofy outfits taking orders. We went to mass today and I swear I smelled cigarette smoke.

After waiting forever, we get our baked potatoes, grab a table, and start to dig in. Anna wants the whole scoop about Howie so I fill her in on every detail. I tell her all about our official first date on New Year's Eve, the awesome way we text each other every day and talk to each other every night. I save the best part for last.

"We're supposed to go out the Friday before Valentine's Day and Jeremy wants to go with you. Like a double-date thing."

Anna screams. People all over the restaurant stare at us.

"Shhh, Anna."

"Okay, like you mean he wants to go with me?"

"Yeah."

"Shut the front door. Did you tell him I'm in?"

"Well, no. I texted you, remember? You didn't want to talk to me."

"No way am I missing this. I'm going. Let's text Howie right now and tell him. Oh my God, I still can't believe you two are dating and you've been texting every day. This is so over-the-top-better-than-awesome."

"Anna, it's not that exciting," I say.

"Yeah, it is. Dish everything." Anna picks up her phone, checking the time. "I mean, everything. And do not leave out your first kiss. Start with the kiss." Anna shoves a forkful of piping hot baked potato in her mouth, waving her hand in front of her face to deal with the heat. She's also giving me the signal to talk.

"We were at the ice rink and he kissed me, I just told you," I say.

"Not what I meant and you know it. I'm talking about *the* kiss, the romantic movie, two minute long, lips totally locked together kind of kiss."

"Hasn't happened yet." I salt my potato, holding up a bite, the steam rising. I decide to put it back and mix it up a little bit so it cools down.

"What?"

"Is there some rule book about kissing? Who says people have to follow a schedule?"

Anna leans over the table. "I thought Madison said you two were making out at Z-man's party." Anna takes another huge bite and sips her Diet Coke to cool off her mouth.

Putting my fork down, I take a drink of Diet Coke. "We were *about* to kiss. The make out scene was total gossip." Seeing the excitement in Anna's eyes, I get all jazzed up too. I forget I'm in the Wendy's and I'm right back in Z-man's house. I tell her the whole story, including the almost kiss in the study. Then I tell her more details about Howie and I ice skating together at the fundraiser, the romantic dinner afterwards, the coffee shop, the text messages from Howie that make me laugh. OMG, I'm scared out of my mind.

"Why does your face look like you're jumping out of an airplane?" Anna asks.

"I'm not sure I can do this," I say.

"Yes you can," Anna says.

"Easy for you to say, you weren't dumped by your first boyfriend."

"Mello, I don't think James is the same thing. He wasn't your first love or first everything."

"How can you say that? You don't think I was in love?"

"You never said you and James were a big deal. Why are you getting so ticked off at me?"

"You don't think I was in love with James? He was my first kiss. *First everything*. Doesn't that mean anything to anyone?"

"Mello, people are staring. Wait, did you say *everything*?" Anna lunges forward. "And *you* didn't tell me that part *either*?"

"No, not *everything* everything. As soon as he realized he wasn't going to get *everything* from me, he dumped me." Anna's face is all blurry.

"Shit. I had no idea. I thought you two were holding hands and giving pecks on the cheek. You didn't tell us. Why didn't you say something? When did he—"

"Dump me? The weekend we all packed up Abby's room. The weekend before she moved away."

"Oh, hey, now I remember. We all slept over at her house both nights. The first night you were gone for a long time."

"Yep."

"You got back when we were getting ready to all crash."

"Yep."

"The next morning, we walked to the donut shop and you were so quiet."

"Ah ha."

I roll my Wendy's napkin up into a ball.

"James is not the same as Howie."

"How do you know?"

"Easy. Did James teach you how to skate? Did James call you every day? OMG, Mello, he's got all the signs."

"Signs of what?"

"Newsflash: boyfriend."

Boyfriend? Love? I take a sip of Diet Coke and try to put the fire out inside my stomach.

"What's the matter?" Anna says as she sticks her head underneath the table. "You jam your toe or what?"

"Let's change the subject."

"You sure? We should probably talk about this. You seem pretty wrecked over James."

"No, I'm okay. I don't want to talk about him anymore." I take a deep breath.

Anna and I go through a quick catch up with our lives. I ask her about the volleyball season and congratulate her on winning the division even after losing to their rivals, something the statistics said they'd never do. Anna asks about my parents and the holidays, of course. I tell her how hard the holidays were and how I had to work at the business for a while. Anna couldn't quite get why working at the family business wouldn't be a blast, but I get where she's coming from. Helping out the accounting department would be super exciting to her. She loves numbers.

"Okay, so let's go back to the Valentine's Day thing. By the way, is *your* Howie aware of what comes after Friday?"

"Anna, he's not *my* Howie and I'm sure he's probably heard of Saturday coming after Friday."

Anna grabs my cell phone sitting on the table.

I reach over. "What are you doing?"

"I am finding Howie in here and texting him. I need to tell him your birthday is on Saturday, February eleventh." Anna's fingers are flying. "Perfect. I told the love of your life *it's mello's b day on Saturday Feb. 11 and hi from Anna who stole mello's phone when she wasn't looking.*"

I've been hiding Howie from my parents. *Shoot.* I need to tell Anna what's going on.

"Anna. My parents had a fit when they found out I went to Z-man's party with Howie and Jeremy, so whatever you do, don't tell them about the Valentine's thing."

"Okay. I don't ever talk to your parents. But if I do, I'm not sure if I can lie. I'm not good at lying. You're seriously telling me you've been hiding Howie? Doesn't he pick you up and drop you off at home?"

"He picks me up at the bakery and I make sure he drops me off after my parents are asleep." I don't confess to Anna that I've been telling my parents I'm out with her.

"Are you nuts?"

"What else am I supposed to do? I'll tell Howie the truth, but I want to wait until he gets to know me better, so he won't think I'm a total loser with crazy ass parents."

Anna stares at me.

"Stop looking at me like I'm a total freak show. So, can we get picked up and dropped off at your house?"

"What about my parents? They're gonna ask why the boys aren't driving you home."

"So we'll make something up."

"I can't lie to my parents."

"It's not really lying. Why don't we tell them we want to have girl talk after our dates?"

"How about you sleep over? This way we can talk about the whole date night afterwards. It'll be fun. But I think you should be honest with your parents. Wouldn't telling the truth be easier than lying?"

"No way. I don't want them to know yet. They'll totally go bonkers and obsess over him. They'll insist on meeting him and wanna have him over for dinner. I wouldn't be surprised if they hired a private investigator and took a sample of his DNA. They're kinda off the deep end with everything I do lately and I want to do this my way, without them getting involved. I'll deal with them soon."

"I wouldn't let this go on for very much longer. Don't you feel guilty for lying?"

"Anna, you're lucky you're not forced lie to your parents to live your life, but I do." A sharp pain slices through me, and I grab my side.

"Are you having a freakin' heart attack? Are you okay?"

"Yeah, I'm fine. I need some ginger ale, that's all."

"I'll drive you to the Mini Mart. If we leave now we can get back to school in time for our next class."

Walking back to Anna's car, our talk about first loves and kisses, my birthday and boyfriends scares the crap out of me. Howie scares the crap out of me. This is all too good, too perfect. I'm sure my life can't go on like this, I'm sure the good's gonna come to an end. I know this isn't her fault, but I tried to do the right thing, tried to make up with Anna and now my life is totally out of control.

I get into Anna's car and click my seatbelt. My phone buzzes with a text from Howie.

bday girl U didnt tell me ☺ i got big plns 4 u

Chapter 15

Reasons why I should stop lying

1. I don't want to hide anymore.
2. I don't like being dishonest.
3. My life is out of control.
4. Cowards lie.
5. I want to be real.

Howie, Anna, Jeremy and I spent the last few days texting back and forth about the weekend. We are totally psyched. I can't wait to go to the *Rocky Horror Picture Show* Friday night and hang out at Howie's house. Then on Saturday, Howie's surprising me and taking me out for my birthday after work. He wants the night to be a total secret. He says I'll love what he's got planned.

I put my phone down on my nightstand and stare at my guitar. Howie and I had a seriously long phone call. He drew the entire time. I could hear the charcoal scratching across the paper. He's home alone every night like me. His parents always work long hours. Since Francesca went to college I've been in the house alone by myself every night during the week. I thought I was the only one with a life like mine. I lie down and turn my head towards Francesca's bed. I wish I could talk to her. I bet if Francesca were here, she'd tell me

Anna's right about Howie not being the same as James. But I'm still afraid. What if things don't work out between Howie and me? Francesca always believed I would find true love and for sure she'd say Howie's like the perfect guy for me and I need to take a chance. I think about Howie and Francesca as I drift off to sleep.

***

Jeremy merges onto the Edens Expressway, headed to Howie's house. I'm sitting in the back with Howie, Jeremy's driving, and Anna's in the passenger seat. The four of us had an awesome time tonight. We went to a movie theatre on the north side of the city near Wrigley Field that plays the *Rocky Horror Picture Show* every Friday and Saturday night. I had no idea what *Rocky Horror Picture Show* was until I watched it on *Glee*. We didn't dress up, but we had a blast trying to sing to the songs and keep up with the dance moves. I don't think I've laughed so hard and so long —ever. The guys were hilarious. Anna and I were a little freaked out about dancing at first, but then the entire theatre was up on their feet dancing on the seats and in the aisles. No one cared about what anyone else was doing. No one cared about looking like a total dork and we had a serious blast.

Howie takes my hand and I don't pull away, for once. My heart starts to race but I don't care. The four of us cannot stop laughing as we replay the night.

Sometimes I think you have experiences in your life where for whatever reason, good or bad, a memory gets drawn into a person's DNA with a permanent marker. Tonight was one of those nights.

Jeremy and Howie give each other a hard time about how they were dancing. Jeremy makes some remark about Howie's figure skating getting in the way of him being able to dance like a heterosexual.

We all laugh and then, *boom.* Howie kisses me. Before I can figure out what's going on, a big blanket gets thrown over me and I'm in a dark, safe place. I hear Anna and Jeremy's voices but I don't care what they're saying. Jeremy shouts something and the blanket gets pulled off. He shouts again.

"Dude. Street or driveway?" Jeremy stops the car.

"Driveway's cool," Howie says, his hand still cradling the back of my head.

As I get out of the car, I swear I'm floating in a swimming pool. Howie puts his arm around me while we walk up to the house.

Anna elbows me and whispers in my ear, "Yaowza."

I elbow her back and nod with a smile.

"Wow. Your house is so cool." Anna points to the white stucco, black shutters and red door. His house is so unlike all the houses in our neighborhood with their same old boring, brick and aluminum siding trying-their-hardest-to-look-good-but-will-always-look-like-crap kinda houses.

Howie walks over to a silver box hanging on the side of a three-car garage. He punches in a code. I pick at a loose thumb cuticle and peek into the window. I spot a grand piano and oversized white couches in a room with a fireplace. I wonder if Howie plays the piano or if one of his parents does. I bet his mom is really pretty.

As the garage opens, Howie takes my hand again and we all walk into his house through a laundry room. We pass a silver ginormous washer and dryer and coats hanging on hooks. On the other side of the room there are two cubbies jammed with workout clothes and sports stuff. Howie leads us into a huge modern kitchen, not quite as big as Z-man's, but close. The countertops are made out of concrete or something I've never seen before. Three metal stools with purple cushions are parked around the end of the counter, which is as big as Giovanni and Rocco's table at the bakery. An ultra modern black leather chair with silver chrome sits in front of a bookcase in the family room, right off the kitchen. The couches are purple and match the stools.

"Be right back. You can throw your coats on a chair." Howie disappears through a door and Jeremy opens the fridge like he lives here.

"Anyone want something? Doctor Mom Goldstein always stocks the fridge with organic shit." He holds up a tray of fresh grass growing out of black plastic containers. "Anyone want a shot of wheat grass?"

"What's up with this?" Anna brushes her hand along the top of the grass.

Jeremy puts the tray back in the refrigerator. "Mrs. Goldstein cuts a section off and blends it up into a smoothie every day. She's sort of a health freak."

Howie comes back and has two bottles of wine or champagne, I can't tell which. He sets them down on the counter, takes his coat off and throws it over one of the kitchen stools. He pops open the champagne, takes four flat-bottomed glasses out of a cabinet and pours, passing the first one to me. When everyone has a full glass, we clink.

"Oh my God, this is sooo good. What is this?" Anna says after she takes a drink.

"Champagne, from France," Howie says.

I take a sip. The bubbles tickle the back of my throat and it tastes really awesome, sort of like bitter ginger ale.

"My aunt lives in France. She sends us cases of wine and champagne for Mom's birthday and every holiday," Howie says.

"Jeremy just said your mother was a health freak?" Anna says.

"She is, but likes to serve champagne for parties and holidays. Which is why we always have a huge stash. My parents will never find out I swiped a few bottles."

"Wait. You have an aunt who lives in France?" I ask.

"Yeah. Totally awesome, right?" Howie says.

"Wow, so cool. You ever been to France?" Anna asks.

"Not yet. One of these days," Howie says.

"Mello, didn't I spot a France brochure in your hands the other day?"

"You going to France?" Howie asks me.

"No way. Just dreaming about going." I put my hand up.

"Let's go downstairs." Howie grabs the bottle and my hand.

"Anyone wanna shoot some pool?" Jeremy asks.

"Anyone want to chalk Anna?" I try to sound snarky.

Howie raises one eyebrow.

I meant Howie should give Anna a blue nose like he did with us at Z-man's party, but the words came out wrong.

Howie squeezes my hand. "I can chalk Anna. How about you? I love this champagne. Here." Howie pours more in my glass.

Jeremy fills Anna in on the joke. When we get downstairs Anna and I cannot believe how awesome Howie's basement is. Jeremy sets the other bottle of champagne down on a coffee table near the pool table.

"Hey, Anna, I bet I can kick your ass in pool," Jeremy says.

"Bet you can't," Anna says.

"You two shoot a game without us. I gotta show Mello something." Howie leads me past the pool table and towards a closed door.

My hand is cradled in his, and my fingertips and my toes are numb from the champagne.

"Welcome to my cave." Howie opens the door. Three easels sit in the middle of the room. One of them has a charcoal drawing of mountains and an ocean. Another easel holds a black and white abstract, the lines super straight and angled. The third easel is empty. Other pencil sketches and some cartoonish drawings are tacked up to the walls. All the wooden chairs in the room are covered in paint splatters.

"Come on in." He sets the bottle down on one of the old wooden chairs.

I walk around, like I'm in some art gallery. "Wow. You didn't tell me you were an Olympic skater *and* an artist."

"I'm not an Olympic skater and everyone's an artist. You're an artist." He puts his arm around my waist. Every time he touches me a bolt of electricity runs through my body.

"Not quite." I chew on my cheek a little.

"Sure you are. Ever try drawing or painting?"

I think about the tree I drew in the closet.

"I doodle, but not much more." I hold up a pastel drawing of mountains and the ocean. "So what's this? Looks like a real place."

Howie puts his glass down. "My parents took me to Hawaii a few years ago for spring break."

"Was that about the best trip ever?" I remember Francesca and I making our big plans of someday living somewhere beautiful.

"Not really," he says.

"What do you mean?"

"I mean Hawaii is paradise, don't get me wrong. But it totally sucked because I was with my parents. I tried to have a good time but after two days I realized my parents were completely insane. I couldn't figure them out. They looked forward to this trip for so long and when we got there, they complained about everything. I signed up for every activity I could at the resort to avoid them."

I start to panic. Part of me wants to run away, but part of me doesn't. I'm ready to take a chance. So I take a few more gulps of the champagne, hoping to drown out the voice inside my head yelling at me to run out of here as fast as I can.

Howie and I walk over to the corner of the room where a big drop cloth spotted with dried paint is laying over a chair. He slides another chair over and sets the bottle down. He takes my hand and we both sit down on the floor. He claps his hands together.

"Okay, so I have something for you, but you have to close your eyes and stick out your hands."

I take a big sip of the best thing I've ever tasted and put my glass down on the floor next to me. "Okay." I wonder what the heck he's got in mind. I feel like I do when I get ready to jump off a high dive. When I stand up there and look down I'm terrified, but I know once I jump in, it'll be fun and I'll float back up to the top no problem—as long as I don't panic.

I close my eyes halfway. "You're not gonna like graffiti my face or something, are you?"

"Nope. It's a Valentine's thing. But don't get all excited. Close your eyes all the way. No cheating."

"Okay." I close my eyes and hold my hands out. I feel a piece of heavy paper in them.

"Okay," he says.

I open my eyes. It's a charcoal drawing of John Lennon's character sketch, just like the one I drew on my guitar. I can't believe he did this.

"Oh my God. Howie. You drew this for me? But I didn't get you anything."

He sits down next to me. "This isn't a big deal. So you like it?"

"I love it." My eyes trace the lines of the charcoal. I'm over-the-top speechless. This is so strange, someone being so thoughtful. I can't believe Howie drew this for me. "No one's ever given me something like this." I hold the paper tight.

Howie takes a swig from the bottle and sits closer to me. "I'm glad you like it."

As I stare at the drawing, this is my chance. I could do something right. I turn to face Howie and find the guts to be honest with him. But before I can even think of what to say, Howie presses his lips onto mine and my brain shorts out. I can't breathe. Or I'm breathing so fast I don't know I'm breathing. It's darkness with light.

The fear, the pain, all the what ifs all disappear—like when you're at the beach and in one second when you're not looking, a big wave comes and washes away the sandcastle you spent all day building, but the wave is so awesome you don't care so you grab your boogie board and ride it out.

After a few minutes, fear comes up behind me and hits me in the back. I pull away. And although I stop the kiss, I can't fight the urge to be close. Howie kisses my neck.

"So you believe in fate?" he whispers in my ear.

"What do you mean?" I whisper back.

"Like, no matter what, we were destined to meet each other?" Howie's eyes are less than an inch from mine.

"I don't know. You?"

"Maybe," Howie's looks at me like he's studying a painting. "I don't know you, but it is so easy to be with you."

"Yeah, I know what you mean."

A voice inside my head screams, *Don't be so scared.*

"You have this classic kind of beauty," he says.

My cheeks fall. "What did you say?"

"Classic beauty. You're a classic beauty, like J-Lo. She's pretty not—"

"Cutesy."

"Exactly. You've been told before."

I sit straight up and grab my stomach.

"You okay? I thought I was giving you a compliment, not making you sick to your stomach."

My eyes blur.

I grab the bottle, take a giant swig and hug my knees.

"What?" He sits closer.

"My sister said that to me."

"She said you were a classic beauty? Sounds kinda weird."

"No, I mean … forget it."

"No tell me, I want to hear," he says.

"I miss her so much." My heart splits open at the sound of my voice saying those words out loud—to Howie.

"Wow, I'm sorry." Howie puts his hand around my shoulder and grabs my hand.

"You two super close?"

"Yeah, like best friends, better than best friends." I stare into his eyes.

Howie reaches over and hugs me, tighter than anyone ever has in my whole life. I rest my head on his shoulder. My head is quiet, for once. I hug him back. I close my eyes tight and we don't say a word.

"So, you terrified?" Howie whispers.

"Of what?" I whisper back.

"Everything."

"Yeah, how did you know?"

"Death does that."

I sit up. "Remember when you were a kid and you'd see a magician do the trick with the cups and the little puff balls underneath? I feel like I used to know the trick, like I had it all figured out, but now, no matter what I do, I can't figure out where the stupid puff balls are."

Howie nods. He's got a hurt look on his face.

I close my eyes then open them. "What? Tell me."

Howie takes a big swig from the bottle, his eyes shift away from me.

He clears his throat. "So, are your parents messed up?"

"Messed up?" I bite my lip.

"About your sister." Howie scratches his head.

"Yeah."

"I hope I don't end up all screwed up like my parents," he says.

"What do you mean?"

"When the twins died, they died. They changed. They're obsessed with finding a cure, like if they could cure the disease, they'd bring the twins back. I mean, I get it, it was a total nightmare."

I grab Howie's hand. "I can't imagine two of them dying. I totally understand why your parents might be a little messed up."

"They had me go live with my uncle for a while, after my brother, they knew it would be a few days or only a week until my sister died."

"Gosh, I don't know what to say." Our eyes lock together and we're connected by something greater than the universe. Like a secret pact only he and I understand.

I wonder how people get through life when awful and evil things happen.

He shakes his head. "I know this sounds crazy, but sometimes I think my mother pretends it didn't happen. She lives her life lying to herself," he says.

He braids his fingers around mine. "I hate when people lie to each other and can't face the truth, you know?"

"Yeah."

We sit for a few minutes and even though total silence fills the room, at the same time the room is filled with sound.

I promise myself no more lies to Howie as our lips touch and we hold on tight and leap into one of his paintings.

Chapter 16

"Mello? Are you awake?" Anna whispers from the top bunk.

"I am awake, but I'm floating. Do you think this is what love feels like?"

"No clue. I've never been in love."

"Me neither."

"Anna?"

"Yeah?"

"This is the first time since Francesca died and I've opened my eyes and she wasn't the first thing I thought about. I feel horrible."

"I think she'd understand. You're thinking of her now, right?"

"Yeah."

"So, what'd you think of first?"

"Howie."

Anna laughs. "Knew it. Francesca would totally understand. You had a hot and heavy make out session with the love of your life. Mello, it was your first real kiss and it lasted all night. You totally lucked out."

I take a deep breath, and hold my hand up in the air, imagining Howie holding it, the two of us lying next to each other. "Yeah, I did, didn't I?" I remember Anna and I talking last night about Jeremy. "Hey, sorry you and Jeremy didn't hit it off quite the same way."

"No joke. I like Jeremy a lot, don't get me wrong. But the kiss. Oh my God. Yick."

I'm on the bottom bunk, so I slide out and plop down on the pink beanbag chair so I can face Anna. It crunches as I sink. I lay my head back, the memory of last night still swirling around me like smoke does in a cartoon. I snap myself out of my love dream and back to reality. I realize what Anna said.

I sit up. "Anna. Was the kiss that bad?"

Anna sits straight up, her head almost touching the sky blue ceiling with puffy white clouds she and her sisters painted one weekend. "Ugh. Soooo bad, Mello." Anna puts her face in her hands, her blond hair hiding her for a second.

She pushes her hair behind her ears. "I mean, how can a guy can be so drop dead cute and be such a *shitty* kisser?"

"Speaking of shitty, your face looks like you just ate shit."

Anna throws her pillow at me and we both crack up. "That's how horrible the kiss was. Just thinking about it makes me want to barf."

I grab my sides, cracking up so hard I can hardly breathe. When we finally stop laughing, we rehash all the details of last night, retelling every moment.

"We totally have to make a list," I say to Anna.

"Awesome idea. What's wrong? You look funny all of the sudden."

"I just realized something."

"What?"

"This will be the first list I've ever made with someone besides Francesca."

"And ..."

"I feel like I'm ditching her."

"Well you aren't. She'd want this for you."

I blink at Anna.

"You can't live in black for the rest of your life, Mello. She would want you to be happy. So you start."

"I'm not in the mood now."

"Fine, I'll start," she says. "One: doing the *Rocky Horror Picture Show* dance." Anna cracks herself up trying to do dance while sitting.

I can't resist her shaking around.

"Okay, two: Howie putting the chalk on your nose."

Anna laughs. "You two totally came out of his cave just so he could do that to me, didn't you?"

"Yeah, we did."

Anna puts her finger up in the air.

"Three: first ever real French champagne," she says.

"Zsa," I say.

"Four: Mello's first kiss."

"Not my first kiss," I say.

"Okay, your first *true love* kiss. So James *the scum bag creep* gets erased from your memory." Anna waves her hand like she's got a wand.

"Five: thankful that Anna's kiss happened at the total end of the night." I point to Anna.

"Oh yeah." She points back.

Anna's phone goes off, blaring some country song. Anna jumps off the top bunk and lunges for her phone. "Shit."

"Jeremy?"

"Yep."

"Mello. Now what am I going to do? This is like going out with Rob Pattinson and he ends up being the worst kisser ever. Oh my

God, I'm totally getting grossed out right now by the thought of his squirmy little tongue." Anna shivers.

I bust out laughing. "Anna, now you're grossing *me* out."

"I'm telling you, it felt like a worm or something."

"Ew. Anna. Stop."

Anna and I hug our sides in uncontrollable laughter.

Anna reads the text and throws her phone down. "He's wondering what I'm doing tonight."

"Anna."

"Mello."

"What are you gonna do?"

"No clue. I loved our double date thing. But I can't kiss him again."

"Tell him you've decided to become a nun."

"Mello. Be serious. I'm in trouble here. This is crisis. Any other non-smart-ass suggestions?"

"Truth?"

We both wince at the same time.

"I'll devastate him. What if some other girl likes the way he kisses'?"

"Yick. What are you gonna do?"

Anna chews on her thumb. "I dunno. I'm gonna ask one of my sisters."

***

Anna pulls into the driveway, and I grab my side.

"You okay? Too much champagne last night?"

"Ugh. My stomach was hurting so bad for a few weeks and then it stopped, but now it hurts so bad I think I might puke."

"So you might want to go to the doctor. What time do you work?"

"Not until noon. Mrs. Sparacini wanted to give me the whole day off because of my birthday, but I insisted on working so Howie could pick me up there instead of dealing with him meeting my parents."

"Mello. Maybe if you stop hiding Howie from your parents your stomachache will go away."

Anna logic alert.

"Anna, I know I have to stand up for Howie, but it's complicated. My parents hated all the guys Francesca brought around so I'm sure they'll hate Howie and we'll end up fighting every day about him."

"First of all, you're not Francesca and Howie is not one of Francesca's boyfriends. And two, judging from that red spot on your neck, I don't think I'd worry about him dumping you."

"What?" I flip the mirror down. "Not funny. I do *not* have a hickey."

Anna points to a tiny red spot behind my left ear. "Here."

"Oh my God, Anna. How did you notice that?"

"I got wicked hickey radar."

"I better start putting makeup on this thing now." I grab the door handle to get out of the car. "Thanks for letting me stay over and stuff."

"No problem. Good luck, Mello. And promise to call or text me with every detail of this birthday date."

"Promise."

***

My mother's in the kitchen filling her go-cup with coffee. She turns towards me with a stern look on her face. Her wrinkles are getting deeper.

"Oh, hi. I'm on my way out to go help set up at the church."

I wonder if the love thing is detectable and shield-like.

My mother's face softens. "You feeling better about things, now?"

"Possible."

"Feeling so good you think you might want to spend a semester in France?"

"What are you talking about?"

"Your guidance counselor called me at the office yesterday afternoon. She wanted to inform me you were declined for a scholarship, but if we were still interested, we should seriously consider a loan. What did you do? Forge our signatures? Why not act like a responsible person and talk to us, Carmella?"

"I don't know. Can I go?"

"Your father and I need to discuss it. Francesca was never interested in any study abroad program."

"So does that mean you and Dad will actually consider letting me go?"

"It depends."

"On what?"

"On a lot of things. On the cost, and if we think you should go."

"So if the cost is reasonable, you'd let me go?"

"If you were looking to do something like this, why didn't you come to us so we could have a conversation? You have to research all your options. I prefer you go to Rome for a semester so you could get more background on the Catholic Church."

"I don't want to learn anything more about the Catholic Church. I want to go to France and learn about the culinary arts, visit the Louvre like once a week and learn about their culture."

"I'm already late. We need to talk about this later, with your father."

"You're making this all about what you want again." I almost lose my breath.

"No, I'm not."

"Yes, you are. Everything always has to revolve around the Catholic Church with you."

"Watch your mouth. There's something to be said for being connected to a faith and being a good person."

"Religion has nothing to do with being a good person."

"Don't get smart with me. I've got to go."

"What are you doing?"

"I'm helping set up the Jesus maze for religious ed. all day. Won't be back until later. Remember, tomorrow we made plans to go to brunch for your birthday after church."

My stomach burns and a searing pain shoots through my middle and up my back. I go over to the cabinet and pull out the industrial size bottle of antacids.

My mother opens the door. "What's with you? Stomach problems or just need extra calcium?"

"Calcium." I chew two up at once.

"You said you're going out with Anna after work, right?"

"Yep."

"We'll talk about this France thing tomorrow. Oh, and your father invited Grandma, Tony, Aunt Maria and Uncle Sol to brunch."

"What? Why?"

"He thought your birthday would be more fun with more people around."

"Shouldn't I be the one to decide who's invited?"

"Carmella. I can't fight about this now. It's not a big deal."

"It is to me."

"I don't think I'll be up when you get home. Don't be out too late." She walks out the door.

My phone goes off in my purse. I think about Howie. I'm shocked to see Donny's number.

"Hello?"

"Hey sweetheart."

Donny only called me sweetheart when he was totally wasted. "Are you okay?"

"I'm better than okay."

"Are you drunk?"

"Nope, I'm drunk and high."

"Donny."

"Sweetheart, I need a favor."

"Where's your sponsor?"

"Dead."

"What?"

"Died in a car wreck. You believe it? It ain't worth it. All that effort to stay clean and sober and boom, he's dead before his time anyway. Listen, I gotta go to the service tomorrow and I need a ride."

"Donny, you need to call another sponsor."

"I don't *need* to call anyone. They're on me like flies on shit. The whole gang of AA people knockin' down my freakin' door. Ach, screw 'em all. I tol' them to get lost."

"Donny, where are you? I'll take you to a meeting."

"Shit. You're just like the rest of 'em. I'm not doin' this. I'll catch you later, sweetheart."

Donny hangs up.

Chapter 17

I spot my mother in the corner of the all-purpose room. She's holding a giant roll of duct tape while another mom stands on a ladder. They're attaching a giant Jesus sign to a string hanging from the ceiling. My mother waves at me, then flashes a fake smile so she can put on her perfect mother act for everyone at the church. She scrunches her face up at me.

She does a whisper-talk when she's a foot away. "What's going on?"

"I tried to call but you didn't answer your cell."

"My phone is in my purse. What happened, what's wrong? You walk here?"

"Yeah, it's only two miles," I say catching my breath.

"What's the crisis?"

"Nothing, I need the car."

"No. You know we don't like you driving. Why aren't you at work? I thought you had to work."

"Mrs. Sparacini gave me the day off for my birthday, last minute. So can I borrow the car for a little while?"

"Carmella, you haven't driven in five months."

"So?"

"The answer is no and I refuse to argue about this here, Carmella."

"But I only need the car for a few hours. I need to help Anna, she's in the middle of a huge crisis. She's always been there for me, helping me out, and for once I want to help her."

"What's wrong with Anna?"

On the walk over, I planned this whole conversation out in my head. "Total wardrobe crisis. Anna's got an interview at the library this afternoon and nothing to wear. Her sisters are all using the car. I only need to use the car for two hours. I'll be back by two thirty the latest. Mom, I'll be careful or I'll make sure Anna drives. If we can't borrow your car, we can't get to the mall and this is a total emergency. She wants this job so bad."

My mother stares me up and down. "Are you sure? Wardrobe crisis? Anna?"

"Yep."

My mother looks around the room and rolls her eyes. "Okay, I'm not going to stand here and make a scene. But you better be back in a few hours. No later than two thirty."

"Fine."

My mother goes over to a long brown folding table full of coats and purses and yanks her purse out from the pile. She dangles the keys in front of me. "Are you okay? You don't look right."

"I'm fine."

"Sure? Your face is awfully pale."

"Probably the fluorescent lights. Might think about some mood lighting for this holy rolling Jesus maze."

My mother gives me the evil eye.

***

I call Mrs. Sparacini from the car while I'm driving. I tell her my friend Anna hurt her finger playing basketball and I'm going with her to the emergency room. Mrs. Sparacini totally understands, wishes me a happy birthday and hopes my weekend is full of big surprises.

Now I'll call Howie. He's at the rink for the next few hours. I hope he's on the ice so I can leave a message.

"Please God, don't pick up. Don't pick up. I promised I wouldn't lie to you and maybe this won't count as lying if I talk to your voice mail."

The sound of Howie's voice on his message makes me want to jump into the phone and tell him that I miss him, I can't wait to be with him, and I'm in total like with him. I'm dying to tell him the truth. I wish I had the guts to tell him about Donny, about how Francesca died, but he'd never understand.

After the beep I tell Howie to pick me up at the coffee shop instead of the bakery. I make up some story about having to deliver some pastries there for Mrs. Sparacini. I'm impressed at how fast I'm making shit up.

After I set the phone back in my purse, I rehearse what I'm going to say to Donny. I've already said these words in my head a million times. They're the words I should have said to Francesca. I know I've been telling lies all over the place this morning, but I'm doing it for a good reason. I need to get Donny to a meeting and then I promise no more lying. When I bring back the keys to Mom, I'm gonna tell her about Howie and never lie again.

***

I pull up to the front of the three-flat brownstone apartment building and lose my nerve. I can't go in. I look up at the front room windows and see Francesca's face. An ax stabs me in the chest as if I just got the news. Since my first date with Howie, the pain in my heart changed into a dull ache, but now I feel like I did when Mom came into my room and announced that my sister was dead. I can barely breathe.

I can't sit here any longer, time is running out. I need to decide if I'm going in, and if not, I need to get back home. Why did I come here? I need to make things right. I need to do this for Francesca. I'm going in.

As I walk closer to the building, I wonder how high and drunk Donny is. I wonder if he's alone or with friends. I imagine a bunch of high, drunk guys in Donny's apartment. My insides vibrate, and my side is aching like crazy, like when I was five and I ran too hard. The ache turns into pings, as if tiny creatures were inside my stomach with pitchforks going at it.

The security door is propped open by three cardboard beer coasters, which is code for someone in the building is having people over, which seems weird for noon on a Saturday. Maybe someone left them there from last night. I buzz Donny's apartment but he doesn't buzz back, so I walk up the steps and knock on the door. After thirty seconds, nothing. Maybe he didn't hear me, so I rap on the door again. Soft voices are coming from inside the apartment, so he's got to be inside. I stare at the peephole. I turn to leave but I can't. I wait for a second, listening to the low murmur of talking and music. I imagine Donny sitting around partying with all their so-called friends who didn't bother showing up to Francesca's funeral. I put my ear up to the door.

The front door buzzer goes off and makes me jump a little. I wonder if my parents sent the cops to come and get me, so I lean over the wooden railing wondering if I'm right.

Luckily, three girls walk through the doorway laughing, carrying huge party store bags and going into the apartment below Donny's.

I rap my fist on the door again.

He's not answering, so I bang three more times. I put my ear up to the door, getting more ticked off, imagining some party scene going on in there. The TV is murmuring and there's some kind of music playing at the same time.

I pound harder. "Donny. Open up. It's me, Carmella."

No sound of footsteps.

What if he's dead?

"Donny. C'mon, open up," I yell and bang on the door as hard as I can.

The door flies open.

I let out a quick scream.

A guy dressed in sweats and running gear stands in the doorway, holding a bottle of water. He's out of breath and sweat pours down the side of his red face.

"What the hell?"

"I'm looking for Donny."

"There's no Donny here."

"He lives here."

"Not anymore."

"He lived here a few months ago."

The guy shakes his head and drinks down half a bottle of water, then wipes his mouth and face with his sleeve. "Are you talking about the dude who used to live here whose girlfriend OD'd in the bathroom?"

My skin is peeling off of me.

I turn around and race down the steps as fast as I can, push the front door open and run towards the bar. Almost out of breath and closer, the bear isn't sitting outside but I keep running anyhow. I get to the door, grab the rotted wooden handle and pull. I step into a totally dark and empty bar. The only sound I hear is the trickle of running water. All the liquor bottles are sitting around the top of the bar and instead of smelling like stale beer, it smells like an indoor swimming pool in here.

The vision of Francesca on the bathroom floor flashes through my brain. I could have stopped *everything* that went wrong that night. My sister would be alive right now if I would have answered her cry for help. But instead, my sister's dead and her life is reduced to "the girl who OD'd in a bathroom" and it's all my fault.

Why didn't I go to the AA meeting with her? How could I be so selfish? I was pissed at her for not returning my calls, but I should have tried to help. I didn't take her to that meeting and now it's too late.

I spot a bottle of whiskey on top of the bar, the kind I used to call the turkey whiskey. Donny, Francesca and I drank it last summer when they were really broke and I'd come down to the city. They did shots with their beer and mixed mine with Sprite.

My arms reach out for the bottle, like they're attached to a string, like I'm a puppet. I grab the turkey whiskey and run out of the bar. I unbutton my coat and shove the bottle into the side, clutching the bottom with my left hand. I race to my car, put the bottle down on the floor in front of the passenger seat and drive as fast as I can towards the lake.

I'm headed to Totem Pole Park, by the harbor where the three of us used to go. At the beginning of summer, Francesca and Donny were living on ramen noodles and Francesca was totally down in the dumps. So one afternoon, I stole a bunch of food from home and surprised them. They were so excited. We went for a picnic at the park, where we could watch the boats go in and out of the harbor. Francesca and I pretended we were on one of them, sailing around the world, rich and beautiful, with husbands who adored us. Right after that day, Francesca slowly started slipping away. At first we didn't talk every day. Then we only spoke three or four times a week, then only once a week. By the middle of August, she wasn't returning my calls. I was so pissed at her. I missed her so bad. She was blowing me off and I had no clue why she was acting so strange. Then she finally reached out to me and I didn't help her.

How could I be such a horrible person?

I park the car facing the harbor and closest to the fake totem pole. I keep the car running for the heat. I pull the bottle out and take a drink, watching the frozen lake, the empty boat slips, and the totem pole dotted with snow in front of me. The whiskey burns my throat, but I don't care. I take another drink, and another. I drink like Francesca did. After my fourth drink, my throat doesn't burn anymore and my fingers start to go numb. I spot another runner, all dressed in winter running gear, her cold breath billowing up towards the sky. Another drink. Each gulp helps pull the knife out of my heart.

I check the time. What happened to Donny? Where is he? I'm scared he's dead somewhere. I grab my phone and dial his number. No answer. I leave him a message and tell him to call me, it's an emergency. I hang up and call right back, leaving another message. I tell him where I am, at our picnic spot by the totem pole and I tell him that I'm pissed he moved out and didn't tell me. I take another big gulp and leave another four messages. I text him eighteen times, then throw the phone down on the seat next to me. My head starts to spin and I realize I need to drive home. I never had to drive after I've been drinking. When I drank with Francesca and Donny, I'd crash on their couch. And I've never had turkey whiskey straight out of the bottle. Stellar day. I don't have a choice. I've got to get the car back to Mom. I'll drive super slow and careful.

As I start to drive out of the park, my stomach erupts and my mouth waters. I taste whiskey. I pull over just in time to open the door and puke up all the whiskey. Frantically, I search for tissues in my purse. After wiping my mouth and blowing my nose a hundred times, I head out of the park.

I drive in the right lane, focused on keeping the car straight and far away from other cars. People beep at me every two seconds. I'm almost to the expressway and my mouth starts to water again. I turn down a side street with all red brick bungalows lining either side. I pull over and puke my guts out onto a curb. I grab my stomach. I think I've been sliced in half with a butcher knife. I look down at the pavement and see bright yellow liquid and red dots everywhere.

The taste of blood fills my mouth and my stomach hurts worse than ever. I lay my head back and try and get my mind off the pain. I need to drive the car back home.

I sit up and squeeze the wheel tight. I head down the expressway, and feel like I might throw up again. I'm not sure if I can make it. I wonder if I should pull over and call my mother but I can't. My parents will kill Donny and me if they find out I was out here looking for him so I chew on Tums while the car bumps along the expressway.

I pass the Pulaski Street exit which means I'm about halfway home. The top of my head is all sweaty and the palms of my hands are sticky. My stomach is cold and hot at the same time. I'm dizzy, so I grab another Tums and start to gag while I chew. I can't puke in the car. I can't stop now, I've got to keep driving, so I pray to God for help.

Dear God,

Since Francesca died, it's been hard for me to be honest with people. So I was thinking I could start trying to be honest with you. A few things have been on my mind like twenty-four-seven, and to be honest, I've been afraid to say these thoughts out loud, because, well, you are God and all.

First of all, I think you hate me. There, I said it. And I wonder if you hated Francesca too. I know she made a lot of mistakes and bad decisions but I don't think it was fair to let her die alone.

Second, I'd like to know why some people have an easier life than others? And what's with this suffering thing? I know what my religion teachers tell me at school, but I don't buy this whole free will theory crap.

And so ever since you took Francesca from us, I wonder if you exist. And if it is true, that you love all of us, why is there such a thing as drugs, addicts, diseases and hate and lies, wars and evil?

Third, I'm sorry for everything I did that was wrong. I'm sorry for lying to everyone all the time but I don't know how to live without lies. It's easier to lie than to tell the truth. Truth is scary. Like now. Saying that I doubt God? If anyone at church or school heard me, they'd run for cover, thinking lightning was going to strike.

To be honest, I think you do exist. I do not understand your ways, and I'm still not buying anyone's theories, but I totally believe in you.

One more thing. Please make sure Francesca's not lonely. And please tell her I miss her and will miss her every day for the rest of my life.

    Love,

    Me

***

Finally, I get to the church parking lot. My body shakes and I'm freezing cold. A sharp pain cuts through my middle, and I lean over a little to try and stop the gun going off in my stomach as I get out of the car and walk up to the church.

I pull the door open to the all purpose room. My mother's back is to me in the corner. As I walk, my legs feel like they're in a bathtub full of ice.

I can't walk too fast. I make my way to where my mother's standing.

She turns around. "Oh my God, Carmella. You're white and shaking. What happened? Were you in an accident?" She puts her hand on my forehead. "Oh my God, you smell like whiskey … and vomit."

"Yeah." I hand the keys to her. "I think I should go to hospital."

"Let me get my purse." My mother grabs the keys from my hand. "Go sit down."

I walk over to a metal folding chair and slide into it. My mother rushes over to me with a few other moms. One of them says, "Gina, she looks like she's in shock. Good Shepherd is right down the street."

All the moms put their hands up to their noses and wince at me. I must smell wickedly bad. This is about the worst thing I could do to my mother.

"Let's go." My mother takes my arm, squeezing it a little harder than she should as she walks me out.

***

I stare at the pale green curtain. The nurse just put an IV in my left arm. She says they need to hydrate me and stop the vomiting, so I'm getting a bag of something. I can't keep my eyes open and my stomach still hurts. As I drift off, I remember the last time I was in the emergency room was when Francesca cut her finger with one of those X-Acto knives. She was working on an eighth grade science project. Blood was gushing everywhere. They gave her five stitches. She hated science.

I force my eyes open and peek over at my mother. She's sitting in the chair next to me, her arms folded across her chest, her legs crossed, her right ankle shaking. She's never been so mad at me.

I can't tell her about Donny, but I'm worried he's in trouble. The tiny pitchfork people are jabbing me in the stomach harder now, so I curl up and squeeze my fists together.

My mother stands up and holds my hand. "Where the heck are they? We've been here for an hour."

"I'm worried about Donny." I close my eyes.

"What?"

"I didn't need the car for Anna. I needed the car so I could go find Donny." I stare at the ceiling, afraid at what mother's face must look like.

"What? Are you crazy? You mean you weren't drinking whiskey with some friends, like normal teenagers who get into trouble hanging around the wrong crowd? Where in the heck did you get your hands on whiskey in the middle of the day? Tell me you robbed a liquor store." My mother reaches into her purse and pulls out her mints. She puts one in her mouth.

I think I might puke again. My mother puts a metal bowl up to my chin as I sit up, but all I do is gag.

Mom rubs my back. I imagine she's shaking her head like she always does when she doesn't get me.

I stick my hand out so she can give me a tissue. I wipe my mouth. "I got the whiskey from the bar where Donny hangs out. He's missing. I went to the apartment, but he moved. He called me, his sponsor died and he wanted a ride to the funeral. He was drunk and high. He sounded like Francesca."

"Carmella, I have no idea what you're talking about. All I know is I lost one daughter to drugs and my other one comes into the church smelling like vomit and whiskey. What did I do to deserve this?"

"Donny got better but then he messed up again. I need to help him find his sponsor. Aren't you always telling us to help people? Aren't I being a good person?"

"Carmella, if you want to help someone, you could help me figure out how to get you to stop obsessing over Donny. What is your problem? We're sitting in the ER because you're throwing up blood. Donny's like a disease, like a cancer. He killed Francesca, I refuse to let him kill you too."

"Oh my God, you don't understand. That's not true. He got me to stop eating Oreos and milkshakes. He got me to start thinking."

"Now I get it. I thought because Francesca was gone, you changed. But now I see, Donny's the reason you've changed. You stop talking to him, or texting, or whatever you're doing, understood?" My mother slides the curtain open and walks out.

A monster alien takes over me and pushes up through my gut. My head is going to pop off my shoulders. I can't believe my mother. I can't believe she would blame everything on Donny. Why doesn't she understand I need to help Donny? Why can't she ever accept what I need in my life?

The curtain slides open, the sound rattling along the metal track makes me jump.

"Carmella, I'm Dr. Nelson."

A doctor with greyish hair who reminds me of Steve Martin walks up to the side of the bed.

He sticks his hand out. "Nice to meet you, sorry for the wait. I'm the gastroenterologist here." He scrunches up his eyebrows. "You look like you're in a lot of pain. I'm going to take care of that right away." Dr. Nelson walks over to the sink and washes his hands.

Dr. Nelson comes back and pushes on my stomach. I wince and grab onto the metal railing with my right hand.

"So I bet you had this pain before drinking too much whiskey. How long have you had stomach problems?"

"I don't know." I can't remember when stomachaches weren't a part of my life. I've had stomachaches my whole life. "A few months, probably," I lie.

Dr. Nelson walks over to the computer, taps on the keys, then reads the notes from the first doctor who checked me in an hour ago. He walks back over to me.

"The nurse will be in shortly. We need to give you a sedative and something stronger to stop the pain, then I'll look into your stomach. Someone your age should not be drinking alcohol. You know that."

"Yes."

"You absolutely need to stay away from it. You'll need to be careful about what you eat and drink for the next year or so. I suspect—"

My mother pushes through the curtain.

"You must be Mrs. D'Agostino." Dr. Nelson shakes my mother's hand.

My mother walks over to my bedside, her left hand grips her purse strap, her right hand is on my arm. She looks like she's gonna jump out of her skin.

Dr. Nelson continues, "Mrs. D'Agostino, I was just about to tell your daughter that I suspect she's got the beginning stages of a mild ulcer. We're going to give her a sedative and examine what's going on. When we see this happen to someone her age, it's usually the result of some sort of psychological trauma. Is there something going on in Carmella's life that would cause a high amount of anxiety?"

"We just lost my older daughter five months ago."

"I'm so sorry, Mrs. D'Agostino. Certainly, that would explain a lot. Some people internalize stress, which is most likely Carmella's case. I would strongly recommend family therapy."

"Oh, well, Carmella has seen a priest."

"How about the rest of the family? Other siblings, her father, you?"

"No other siblings and Carmella's father and I don't need therapy. We're very active in the church and have plenty of support within our church family."

"Okay, but if you change your mind, here's the name of someone." Dr. Nelson scribbles a name down on his prescription pad and hands it to my mother. "Carmella will be very out of it tonight, but should be back to normal by tomorrow. The main thing is to make sure she takes her medicine and follows the prescribed diet."

Mom nods, then shoves the piece of paper into her purse.

How to humiliate my mother royally

1. Drink whiskey, since she thinks only alcoholics and addicts drink whiskey.
2. Drink whiskey in the middle of the day.
3. Drink whiskey in the middle of the day and come into the church, in front of all her church lady friends reeking like whiskey and puke.
4. Tell her you were drinking whiskey in the city, looking for Donny and you drove home drunk.

***

Mom helps me into the house. My legs are rubber from the drugs the doctor gave me so he could stick some long black tube thing down my throat. I look at the clock on the microwave. Four fifty. Donny. Howie. Where are they? I need to talk to both of them.

"Four fifty."

"What?" my mother asks.

"Howe's at the coffee shop. I got to talk to Donny."

My mother's face looks royally confused, like she has no idea what I'm saying. I'm talking, but my words are coming out all jumbled. I feel gooey and fuzzy all over. Mom's rattling off something about clear liquids tonight and the medicine she's going to pick up.

"Four fifty. I need to call."

"Carmella? Did you hear me?"

"What?"

"I said I'm going to help you get into your pajamas, then I'll get your stomach medicine and come back. You need to sleep."

I lean on the kitchen chair. "Donny. I told you, find Donny. Call him."

"You've been mumbling over and over since they put you in the car and I have no idea what you're saying. All I keep hearing is how. How what?"

"He'll be there at five."

"You keep saying that too. Boy, they gave you enough sedative for a gorilla."

My mother takes me by the arm and walks me up the steps. I'm so weak and I don't care about anything but sleep. I see my guitar and blurt out Howie's name.

"Who's Howie?"

"My phone." I grab for my purse, but it's not on my shoulder.

"Your phone is in your purse downstairs."

"Gimme."

"For what?"

"Have to call."

"You are not calling anybody right now. You need to sleep." My mother sits me down on the bed and gets my pajamas out of a drawer.

I stick my hand out. "I gotta."

"Your pajamas are on your bed next to you."

"I need the phone now or it will be too late."

"All right already. Boy, when you get stuck on something you don't stop. Okay, I'll call. Who? Anna?"

"Let me."

"Okay, you call, but I'll stay here. She won't understand a word you're saying."

"No, not Anna."

My mother disappears.

She comes back, my cell phone in her hand. "I already dialed Anna for you. Make it fast. I need to get your medicine. And your father is on his way. He'll be home before I get back."

I grab for my phone and miss.

My mother puts my phone up to my ear. "Here, Anna's not answering. You want to leave a message?"

I nod. "Can't go tonight. Call How. Tell him. My stomach. I messed up. Call me. They gave me stuff for a gorilla."

"Oh, geez." My mother takes my phone. "What's with this how thing?"

"You don't know him. Give it back."

My mother puts the phone on the nightstand. "I'm not leaving till you put your pajamas on and crawl in bed. If you don't, I'll take the phone away. And you need to tell me why you keep saying how."

I pull my pajamas close to me and with every ounce of energy I have, I try to pull my shirt off but can't.

"Oh, never mind. You need help."

"Humph."

My mother helps me get dressed. My head is full of water and I don't have any bones in my body. I'm nothing but a watery head attached to a rubber band. I don't care about anything but sleep so I fall onto my pillow.

My mother puts my covers over me. She kisses the top of my head.

"Mom?"

"Yeah?"

"Stay with me?"

"Sure."

My mother sits down on my bed.

I reach for her hand. She cradles mine in hers.

"I'm sorry."

"I'm sorry too, Carmella. Seeing you with that thing down your throat, I realized we need to figure out a better way."

"I love him."

"Who?"

"Howie."

"Howie? Who's that?"

"I met him at the bakery."

"A customer?"

"Yeah. I didn't want to, he made me."

"Oh my God, now what? He made you do something you didn't want to do?"

"Yeah."

"Oh my God, Carmella, don't tell me. I can't handle thinking anything bad happened to you."

I pull on her sweater. "No no no, all good. Not bad. I dinndt wanna fall in total like with him but I did. Shhh. Keep a secret. Maybe I love him even. He doesn't know. Don't tell him. Gotta call him for me. He's supposed to take me out for my brrirthday. I think I love him."

"Oh, Carmella, I'm not sure what you're talking about. We'll talk tomorrow."

My mother rubs my forehead.

"He drew me a John Lennon picture. We have so much fun. He skates and isanartist. I don't think you and Dad love each other anymore. That's why it hurts. You don't love each other and you can't love us anymore either."

"Carmella, stop. We love you."

"Monn, I lost Donny. You need to find him for me."

"Carmella, they gave you way too much stuff. Shhhh. You need to go to sleep now."

"They didn't give me too much stuff. Donny left. He was all straightened out, then he moved, now he's pushing the wagon, or fell off? I dunno. I went to the apartment but he wasn't there. Some runner guy was. He said some girl OD'd in the bathroom. It hurt so bad to hear him talk about Francesca like that. I have to tell you. And you have to love Donny. Francesca loved him. We have to help him for her. Find him. I promised her."

"Carmella. Go to sleep. I'll talk to your father."

"Please?"

"I promise I will talk to your father about finding Donny. But I don't know where he'd be, I don't think we could find him."

"The bar by the street has a bear outside. Like in the woods. Maybe he's in the hostiple or something. I can't staaay awake anymore. Call Howie. Tell me I'm sorry. I mean him."

My mother gently rubs my forehead and side of my head.

I whisper, "I'm sorry."

"It's okay."

I feel her kiss my cheek.

Chapter 18

What truth is

1. Truth is real.
2. Truth doesn't lie.
3. Truth gives you what you need.

I hear *tap tap tap*. I open my eyes. Wet, thick, icy snow slaps against my bedroom window. I roll over. My clock says nine thirty. My head is so heavy, I can hardly lift it off the pillow. My insides have been pulled and stretched, tied in a knot and used like a giant rubber band. The last thing I remember from yesterday was a nurse who gave me something in my arm. My right arm has a Band-Aid on it where they usually take blood. I remember the doctor told my mother and me they were going to stick a camera down my throat to see what's going on with my stomach and if some kind of weird bacteria is causing all my stomach problems.

Howie.

I sit up and almost fall over. I guess I can't move too fast. I reach for my University of Illinois sweatshirt lying on the floor, holding onto my head to try to keep my balance. Dad bought both Francesca and me a sweatshirt when we visited the campus several years ago. Francesca wasn't interested in University of Illinois at all and her grades weren't good enough to get in, but Dad insisted we go get a tour anyhow. His plan was for Francesca to go to a junior college, get her grades up and transfer there so she could go into business and take over Perfection someday. That was his plan. Her plan was to go to California College of the Arts in San Francisco, California. She ended up at DePaul University and she majored in Liberal Arts.

My phone is not on my nightstand so I check my purse. Not in there. I have to call Howie. *Oh my God.* I imagine him sitting in the coffee shop waiting for me last night.

I pull my door open and walk down the steps.

I walk into the kitchen. My mother's standing at the counter writing out a check, my father's at the back door, his hand is on the doorknob. They're arguing about when to reschedule my birthday lunch with the family and being late for church.

"Carmella." My mother walks up to me, puts her hands on my shoulders, and leads me to the chair. "Sit down, you still might be weak. How is your stomach?" She rubs my forehead.

"Where's my phone?"

"In my purse," she says.

"Can I have it back?"

"Not until we talk. We're late for church. We'll be back in an hour."

"What? You're kidding, right? You're going to take my phone away like I'm twelve?" I remember Howie and Donny. "Did anyone call? How long have you been holding my phone hostage?"

"We've had your phone since you got home from the hospital."

I remember telling my mother about Donny. She acts like she might know something, so I ignore the fact that my father's in the room and will probably pound me into the ground for asking, but I have to find out what happened to him.

"Donny. Did he call me? Did he call to say he's okay? Did he leave me a message?"

"No messages from Donny on your phone," my mother says.

"What the hell is she doing?" my father says to my mother. "Why is she talking to him?"

"Why don't you ask her. She said something last night about Donny getting his life back together and now he's missing, probably back on drugs." My mother nods her head towards me.

"I couldn't care less if he's missing. I hope he's dead on the street somewhere with rats chewing on his face. Let's go, we're late for church."

My mother grabs her purse off the counter. "We'll talk about this when we get back. The list of what you can eat is on the fridge. Then go back to bed and rest. You need to heal. The doctor said to keep an eye on your stress."

"If you really cared about me or Francesca, you wouldn't take my cell phone away, and you wouldn't talk about Donny like that."

"We have to make some changes around here. The doctor said the situation with your stomach isn't normal for someone your age. We need to help you stop internalizing everything."

"So you think taking my phone away will change me?"

"Yes, we do."

"We need to go," my father says.

I glare at my father. "You're treating me like a dog. This is going to help? You don't care at all about what I want."

"You're too young to know what you want."

My father and mother walk out the back door.

I bang my fists on the table, and go over to the house phone, which is perched on its charger in the corner of the counter. I have to call Howie. I wonder if he talked to my parents last night, or if he sat in the coffee shop, thinking I blew him off. *Shoot.* His phone number is in my phone. I call Anna.

My stomach is empty and raw. I read the list of what I can eat on the fridge and throw two pieces of bread in the toaster while I listen to Anna's voice mail. I leave a desperate message for her to call me as soon as she can.

While I chew on my toast, I pray for Anna to call me back. I look up at the clock and realize Anna's at church with her family. She's got her phone off. I leave a message for her to call me after mass.

Almost choking on my dry toast, I decide I need to talk to Howie and I need to find Donny and if I'm going to do those two things, I better shower up and steal my mother's car before they get home.

***

I'm still weak, but the shower helped wash some of the fogginess out of my brain and the toast helped too. I'm going to wear my green cargo pants and black long sleeve shirt. I stitched peace signs onto the top of the sleeves like military patches and around the waist I stitched a chain and dog tags. I lace up my black boots, and am going to talk to Howie first. Besides, the bar doesn't open until noon and I can't think of where else to search for Donny.

I put all my rings on and get my coat, then pluck my mother's keys from the giant wooden key holder nailed to the wall. As I open the back door, the doorbell rings.

I turn around. My gut tells me it's Howie.

I walk to the front door and peer through the peephole. He's standing on the front stoop with a giant bunch of red roses. I wonder if my parents talked to him last night and some miracle happened and they had a huge change of attitude while I was passed out. I wonder if Howie didn't get my message from Anna until after he sat in the coffee shop for hours waiting and he's ticked at me.

I take a deep breath and open the door. "Oh my God, Howie." I grab Howie and hug him. "Did Anna call you? Were you sitting in the coffee shop forever last night?"

"No, only like ten minutes before Anna called me. Said you were royally drugged up. She said you said something about a gorilla?"

I laugh louder than I should. "Oh my God. Oops. I don't remember. I remember trying to call her but my mother had to dial."

Keys dangling from my pinky, I need to get away from this house before my parents get back, in case they make a scene in front of Howie. I'll convince him to go somewhere.

"You want to head over to the Elmwood coffee house?"

"I don't think so. Besides, I thought you had stomach surgery yesterday?"

"Not surgery. They did a little biopsy thing is all. I'm fine, not a big deal. So Anna told you the whole story? I haven't even talked to her yet." I ignore the ping in my stomach.

"Your mom called me and said you were seriously sick. She said you were probably going to be in bed for a week."

My brain explodes. Pieces of it hit the backs of my eyeballs.

"You talked to my mom? She totally exaggerates. What else did she say?"

"She said she was 'beside herself' and worried about you."

Howie's tone scares me.

"And?"

"Carmella, we need to talk."

Howie sounds pissed, but I'm not sure because I'm still foggy from all the medicine.

The snow starts falling onto the ginormous bouquet. "You wanna come in? I should probably get those inside before they freeze out here."

"Good idea," Howie says.

I hold the door open. He walks in, hands me the flowers and stands on the foyer carpet. I want to tell Howie he's the first person to ever give me flowers and getting two dozen red roses makes me feel like he just handed me the original Mona Lisa or something.

"Wow, these are nice," is all I can manage to get out.

I decide not to panic at my lack of enthusiasm. I'll tell him how much I love the flowers in a few minutes, after we sit down.

Howie seems mad at me, but at the same time he brought me two-dozen red roses in a glass vase. I should ask him what's wrong, but I'm afraid.

"I'm gonna put these in my room, be right down."

"You mind if I come up?"

Howie being in my house, seeing where I live and grew up is strange, like he's looking in my underwear drawer or something and now he's going to see the room I shared with Francesca.

"Sure, if you want. But don't expect much." I try to sound like this is no big deal to me.

Howie takes off his shoes. I think it's a little weird he asked to come up to my room, but I don't say anything. We walk up the steps. I set the flowers down on my dresser, then notice the huge pile of clothes on the floor. In total panic mode, I shove everything into my closet and pull the closet door closed.

"Your room, huh?"

"Um, yeah." I'm a little out of breath and dizzy. I moved way too fast.

Howie points to my guitar right away. "Hey, didn't I ask you if you played guitar and you said no?"

"Oh, well, I like to surprise people."

"You draw this?"

"Yeah."

"Guitar player and you can draw pretty good."

"Me? I'm not that good."

"Yeah you are. Look at this, all done with a marker? You totally have talent." Howie picks up my guitar and checks out the sketch. "You said you were a doodler and that was it when we were in my cave."

"I didn't think master doodler counted as art."

"Are you kidding?" Howie puts my guitar back down and notices the drawing he did for me tacked up on the wall behind the stand.

Howie reaches for my hand. I'm scared, like he's going to tell me he never wants to see me again. I try to smile the fear away.

"So, that side hers?"

"Yeah."

"Interesting."

"What?"

"Well, I, I don't know. Nothing."

"No, what?"

Howie looks into my eyes. "You want me to be honest?"

"Yeah."

"Isn't that sort of weird?" Howie turns towards Francesca's bed.

I take my hand back and sit down on my bed. "No, not at all. I mean, when she moved out we kept her bed in here. She's in a different time and space now and I don't want to change this room."

Howie nods. He sits down facing me, his knee up on the bed. "So, what's with the stomach thing? You missed out on a big surprise I spent days and days planning and scheming."

"Oh my God, Howie. You didn't. Did you? Shit. I'm such an idiot."

Howie laughs. "Relax. Just yankin' your chain. I did plan a big surprise, but no big deal, maybe another time."

"Oh." My face turns colors. "Sorry."

"Hey, not your fault."

Howie's foot is shaking, like Mom's was at the hospital. He can't sit still. Things are different between us. This doesn't feel like it usually does. He's joking around, but he's not acting right. I wonder what happened last night. I rub the top of my ring, scared of what Howie's thinking. Howie takes my hand. "So, serious. What's up with the stomach?"

"Serious. Just a little sore is all. I'm fine. Doc says to lay off the tacos and chili for a while."

Howie holds onto my hand a little tighter so I firm up my grip too. Maybe things will be all right. Maybe he's worried about me.

"So what happened to you? I mean, how did a small stomach thing turn into a huge emergency?"

I can't tell him I was looking for Donny. "I've been kind of having these bad stomachaches for a while and yesterday I had a pain so bad I couldn't stand up and then I started puking, so my mother put me in the car and yup, that was it."

"Your mother said the doctor told her you could have bled to death."

"Oh my God, she's totally overreacting. She's so paranoid."

"She also said she had no idea we were seeing each other."

I look up at Howie. "She did?"

"Yeah, so the night when you wanted me to drop you off down the street, I'm guessing that was all a story—your mother being sick. She wasn't really sick, right?"

I'm about to make up another lie, but get my courage back and tell him the truth. "Sorry. I didn't want to deal with my parents weirding out until I was sure about everything."

"So when were you going to tell me we were sneaking around behind your parents' backs?"

"Now. Like after the weekend."

"I thought we were honest with each other."

"We are."

"Your mother also told me you're going to France."

"Well, news to me. The last time I checked with them, they said no way."

"You didn't tell me you wanted to go to France. You said you were just looking at the brochure. But according to your mother, you're going."

"Okay, I *do* or *did* want to go to France." I twist my hands together.

Howie stands up. He rakes his fingers through his hair.

I stand up. "Howie. This is not a big deal. I didn't tell you about France because my parents told me I couldn't go. They must have changed their minds and told you before they told me. Honest."

"Nice try. But that's not the point."

"What's not the point?"

"You don't think this is a big deal, do you?" he asks.

"What?"

"You haven't been straight with me about anything."

"We've only been out on a few dates."

"So, the longer you date me, the more honest you'll be?"

"Well, yeah," I say.

"Yeah, see that doesn't work for me."

"What are you talking about?" I fling my arms up in the air.

"I live with parents who lie about the truth of their life every day. They can't be truthful about anything, and I don't even know who they are anymore."

"Oh my God, Howie. I'm not like that. I'm not lying about who I am. Besides, it's not like we're boyfriend and girlfriend yet."

"So what are we?"

"I don't know, good friends?" I rub my forehead. My whole life is out of control. I'm stuck on a sled racing down a hill and I have no idea where I'm going and I can't stop.

"Wow, I thought the night in my cave was more than being friends. Guess it wasn't for you."

"No, you're wrong." My throat closes up, my eyes sting. I have to tell him how I feel, he's slipping away. "The night in your cave was the best night of my life."

I want to scream *I haven't been able to talk to someone like that since Francesca*, but the words won't come out of my mouth.

"So why didn't you tell me you play the guitar?"

"Because I don't anymore. I haven't been able to play since I got the call about my sister."

"What else haven't you told me?"

"Nothing. I haven't lied about anything else."

"Your mother said your stomach was pretty bad, but then I show up here and you're dressed like you're ready to go out. What's the truth, Carmella?"

"This is the truth. Right here. I'm not lying."

Howie looks me in the eye. "I don't know. I swore I'd never be with someone who wasn't totally honest with me. If you can't be honest in the beginning, you won't be honest with me later."

I grab my side.

"And so what next? You don't have a sister who died? Was that all a lie too?"

"You think I would *lie* about my sister dying?"

"I don't know, what do you want me to think? You've been lying about everything else. Who keeps their dead sister's bed in their room?"

"You need to leave."

"Yeah, I do."

Howie walks towards the door.

I hear my mother yell up the steps. "Carmella?"

She gets to my doorway and almost runs over Howie.

My mother's face looks like she saw me jump in front of a train.

"What's going on here? I told you the doctor ordered you to rest. What are you doing all dressed like you're going out? And who is this?"

"What are you doing home? Where's Dad?" I wrap my arms around me.

"We came home right after mass. We didn't stay to talk with Father like we usually do."

Howie flips his keys. "I'm Howie."

My mother glances over at the ginormous bunch of red roses on my dresser. "Oh."

I stand up. "It's so nice you informed Howie I was going to France, Mother. When were you going to tell me?"

My mother takes a deep breath and rolls her eyes. "We were going to surprise you at your birthday dinner. I invited Howie to come celebrate with us too."

Howie and I stare at each other.

My mother looks at the two of us, pushes her hair behind her ear, then looks Howie up and down. "What's going on?"

"I have to go," he says.

Howie's words hit me in the stomach.

I follow Howie down the stairs, dragging my feet.

I watch him put his shoes on. My whole body aches, worse than my stomach. I don't say another word and put on an act for him like this is no big deal. I refuse to admit I'm dying inside. I want him to stay, forever. I love him. But he's going to end up leaving me at some point, so better get the hurt over with now.

I open the door.

He stops for a second like he's going to say something, then turns back around.

I think he's going to grab me and tell me he understands all my little lies. But he doesn't. I close the door, and peek through the front window. He gets into his car and drives away, the snow so thick I lose him in a white blur.

My parents stand in the foyer, both their arms folded.

My father rubs his forehead, turns around and walks into the kitchen.

"You two must love this."

"Carmella." My mother takes my shoulder.

I whip myself away from her and race up to the top of the steps. "I hate you," I scream at my mother from the top of the steps. I want to throw nails at her head.

"We have to talk about this," she says to me.

"Talk about what? How could you tell him I'm going to France?"

"We were going to surprise you. I didn't know he was going to tell you first."

"Yes you did. Now you're lying to me. I wonder where I get this lying thing from."

"Carmella, your father and I want you to go to France."

"Why the hell would you want me to do something that wasn't your idea? That wasn't, God-forbid, church related."

"Because we decided you should get away from here." My father shouts so loud the walls almost vibrate. His eyes are all glassy.

"Get away from here, why?" I try to shout louder than he did.

My father shakes his fist in the air. "To get some relief."

"You made me sound like a liar, like I lied about France and now Howie hates me."

"Well, if that's all it took for him to walk away, then he doesn't care about you," Dad says.

I wipe my face. "He left because of you. This is your fault. Because you two are crazy, I lied about stuff and now he's gone." I spin around and race into my room and slam the door. I grab the red roses off my dresser and stomp over to my window. I put the vase down on the floor, and push the sticky wooden window open. I pick up the vase and start to throw the stupid roses out, but something stops me.

My hands are locked around the vase. This is how Francesca felt. She didn't fight. She thought she was fighting, but throwing people away isn't fighting, it's giving up. She gave up. She gave up on her life, on me, on everyone and everything. For whatever reason, she threw it all away. My knees buckle under me. The snow is getting thicker. The cold wind blows snow through the window and I feel Francesca next to me.

I hug the flowers and scream as loud as I can while I rock back and forth. "I hate you. I hate you for being so scared. Why didn't you let me help you? What did you do about your life? Nothing. Why, Francesca? Why couldn't you fight, just a little bit? I hate you for giving up."

My mother storms into my room and races over to the window. She tries to slam it shut, but the window refuses to close all the way. My father's behind her.

"Carmella. Oh my God, look at you." My mother reaches for me.

"Leave me alone," I shout. I hug my knees closer to me and inch my way into the corner. "Leave me alone. Why do you hate me so much? Because I didn't tell you about Francesca?"

"What? What are you talking about?" my mother asks.

"I knew she was in trouble. I knew she was drinking too much and I knew she and Donny were doing drugs, but she didn't want me to tell you so I didn't. Now you can hate me."

"He forced you to keep quiet, didn't he?" My father bends down slow, so his eyes meet mine.

"No, it wasn't Donny. It was all Francesca and me. It's our fault. I was scared of her, of you. I thought if I didn't tell you, it would go away. I thought someday she'd get her life on track and everything would be all right. The three of you seemed to hate each other and I was afraid you'd grow to hate me too if I told you what was going on."

My mother starts crying. "Carmella, what are you talking about? We love you. We loved Francesca. Oh my God, you've gone crazy keeping all of this bottled up inside." She reaches for me again.

"I said don't touch me." I swat the air.

I grab the vase and cradle the roses in my arms, the last of Howie.

"Carmella, pull yourself together." My father slams the window completely shut, then reaches his hand out. I stare at my dad's hand and remember when things were different with him and me, when his outstretched hand meant he needed me to give him the hammer or the nail or whatever we were fixing. I want to go back to that time when we'd go to the hardware store to get what we needed so we could hang a picture or fix the sink or trim the lower branches of the pine tree in the front yard. I want to go back to a time when our whole lives weren't about trying to fix Francesca.

"No, I'm tired of you treating me like I'm Francesca. She's gone and I'm here. I don't want you to hate me anymore."

"I don't hate you, don't say that," my dad says.

"Carmella." My mother inches closer. "We love you, we're terrified of losing you. I wish you would have told us how much you were hurting."

My father sits down on Francesca's bed for the first time since we got the news. He looks around the room. He runs his hand along the bedspread.

My mother wraps her arms around her waist and shakes her head.

I get up and put my coat on, grab my purse and the keys that are still on my dresser.

My stomach medicine is on my nightstand and I check the bottle, popping one in my mouth and swallowing it, then throwing the bottle in my purse.

"Where are you going?" My father gets up.

"I'm going to try and help Donny."

"Carmella, you need to rest," my mother says.

"I need to do this. I need to live my own life and make my own decisions."

"But, Carmella." My mother gets up and walks over to me.

"Why can't you understand I need to help Donny? That I need to do this for Francesca? And you can't keep treating me like this."

"Like what?"

"Like I'm her. I can't get out of the shadow of her royal screw-ups and I'm tired of it. Just because she made all the wrong choices and decisions doesn't mean I will."

"You think you're making the right decision now? Running out of here and chasing down Donny?" my dad asks.

"You think I should be like her and give up?"

My mother takes my phone out of her pocket and hands it to me.

"Did you read every text? Listen to every message?"

"Yes, we did," my mother says.

I take the phone from my mother's hand. "I've been so wrapped up in feeling guilty for not trying to help Francesca, but I just realized something. Why didn't she ask you for help?"

My mother's eyes glass over. "Or why didn't we accept the reality she was in serious trouble? Why didn't we face the truth?"

My dad gets up off the bed. "C'mon. I'll drive you."

Chapter 19

What to do when your life blows up in your face

1. Fight.
2. Never give up.
3. Adjust your attitude.
4. Stand tall.
5. Believe in yourself.

We're a half block from Grizzly's. The bear is wearing a red bandana.

"You don't have to do this," Dad says.

A black pickup truck pulls out of a spot across the street from the front door.

"Park in that spot." I point. "I'll see if he's in the bar." I take a sip of ginger ale. Mom insisted I bring it along.

Dad turns the ignition off. "If you're not out in ten minutes, I'm going in."

I get out of the car and walk across the street. I slip on the step as I pull the giant wooden door open. The same stale beer and rotting wood hits me in the face, just like before.

Four guys sitting on bar stools turn their heads as I walk in. A guy bartender walks up to me as soon as I approach the bar.

He spreads his hands out on the bar. "You order food to go or what?"

"No, I'm looking for someone."

The bartender shakes his head. "You can't sit here."

"Yeah, okay." I spot Donny sitting at the end of the bar.

As I walk towards him, I can see he's in bad shape. I've seen him really drunk and high before, but his face is so pale, his eyes are bloodshot and he's got dark circles under his eyes.

He's got a tall glass of ice water and a cup of coffee in front of him.

"Donny."

"Try and get him out of here. I cut him off an hour ago. He won't leave." The bartender wipes his hands on a towel.

"Hey, sis." Donny cracks half a smile.

"Donny, let's go. You have to go to an AA meeting. We need to find you a new sponsor."

"I don't need a friggin' sponsor." Donny's smile goes away.

"Donny, let me help you."

"You're the one who needs help."

"Donny, you need to go home."

"I live right down the street. I'll go when I'm ready."

"You don't live down the street anymore. I went to the apartment and some stranger opened the door and scared the shit out of me."

"I live at The Arms now, on the corner."

"That skuzzy place up on North and Sedgewick?"

"Total paradise. Just me and the roaches."

"Donny, let's go."

"I'm not goin' anywhere."

The bartender towers in front of Donny. "Let this girl get you outta here, or I'm callin' the cops. I don't want to, Donny, but you're not good for business. Go."

Donny straightens his body and lifts himself slowly off the stool. "Shit, all you people are a pain in the ass."

We walk out of the bar. "Donny, my dad's parked across the street. We'll give you a ride home." I figure if I can get him in the car, we can take him to the hospital.

"I'm walkin'," Donny says.

"No you're not."

We walk out of the bar.

"I'm going home." Donny points to the corner.

"Donny, let us give you a ride."

"No way, I told you I'm walkin'," Donny snaps at me.

I'm not sure what he might do. "I'll walk you home." I'm scared Donny's gonna beat the shit out of me, but I'm not giving up.

"Get the hell away from me. I'm coming off a three-day bender and I haven't had a drink in hours. You're messing with a real grizzly here."

"But Donny, you need help. You can't give up."

"Face reality, sweetheart. Time to move on. I'm onto what you're doin' and it ain't gonna work. Trying to save me won't change what happened to Frannie. We're all gonna die sometime, so get lost."

Donny starts walking down the street, snow kicking out from under his feet. I turn and run back to the car. Dad's leaning on the driver's side door with his arms folded in front of him.

"I'm going to walk him home," I say to Dad.

"I'll follow you." Dad puts his collar up around his face.

Donny and I shuffle through the snow two blocks without saying a word. I quickly glance back to make sure Dad's behind me.

When we get to the entrance of the old building, Dad grabs my arm. "Okay, let's go," he says.

"Hey, we got ourselves a family field trip," Donny says.

"She wanted to make sure you were okay. Let's go, Carmella," Dad says.

"No. I want to talk to Donny, alone."

"Carmella, you can't go into a place like that."

I pull my coat up to cover my mouth and nose so I don't puke from the stench.

"Ten minutes. Give me ten minutes."

My dad takes a deep breath. His eyes shift from me to Donny and back to me. His hands poke through his pockets.

"Fine, but I'm following you in, and I'll wait outside his door. Ten minutes max."

"You're welcome to join the party, Mr. D.," Donny smirks.

"No thanks, Donny," Dad says.

Dad cups his hand over his nose as we push the door open. This glass paned dirty mosaic tiled entryway must double for a toilet for the homeless in the middle of the night.

Donny, my dad and I walk past an old metal elevator and down a dimly lit hallway. The carpet is hard and crunchy. The walls are cracked and used to be pale yellow. Donny stops at a fake wooden door that has the number 26 in gold numbers on it. He puts the key in the doorknob. He turns the wobbly, scratched brass knob and opens the door. It's dark inside. He flicks a switch and a round fluorescent light in the ceiling splatters on.

My dad gives me a stern look as I follow Donny in and close the door. The first thing I notice is a little refrigerator on top of a brown chipped dresser. I don't know what dying feels like, but if I did, I think it might feel like this room. The fake wood on the nightstand is chipped and the gold and brown flowered bedspread probably hasn't been washed in decades. The curtains are brown and orange striped and have stains on them.

Donny throws his keys down on the nightstand and turns around with eyes barely open. He's creeping me out. He blinks a few times. "Just like home, huh?"

I don't know what to say or do, so I stand in front of the bed, wondering how someone could live in a place like this.

Donny flops onto the bed and turns the TV on and with the remote still in his hand, he closes his eyes.

I sit down. The corner of the bed crumples under me. Donny looks so bad, so worn out.

After a few minutes, I find the guts to talk.

"Donny?"

"What?" Donny says without opening his eyes.

"Can I talk to you for a second?"

"I'm listenin'. Just tired. It's been a rough bender. What day is it?"

"It's Sunday. The Lord's Day."

"Ha." Donny smiles.

I knew he'd smile at that one. He used to make comments about Sunday being the best day to get drunk. He never felt guilty if he blew the day getting drunk or high because it was God's designated day of rest. The Lord's Day, he'd say.

"Donny, I want you to get help. You can't give up, like—"

I can't say it.

"Then consider this my break. Go home," Donny says.

"I can't."

Donny opens his eyes halfway. "Did you come to rescue me or are you running from something?"

"I came to rescue you."

"I told you, forget about me. I'll get help when I'm in the mood to sober up. Something must have happened in the D'Agostino house for your dad to escort you here."

"Yeah, my dad feels sorry for me because I'm so heartbroken about Francesca. I was so mad at her and now she's dead and I can't say I'm sorry. I'd give anything to turn back time, so I could do the right thing."

"You did the right thing. You're human. She pushed you away and you reacted. Quit beating yourself up. She wouldn't want you to keep punishing yourself. You guys loved each other."

"You don't think I'm a horrible monster?"

"You're not a monster at all. Let it go."

"I don't know. I'm so messed up, I totally blew it with a guy."

"A guy you like?"

"Possibly love."

"What the hell are you doin' here? Go get him back."

"I can't."

"Yes you can."

"No, I can't. I'm a liar. I lied about everything. Then yesterday, I stole a bottle of whiskey from the bar when I was looking for you. I got drunk and went to the church. I embarrassed my mother and my father. They tried so hard to cover up Francesca's problems, and then I go and show up in front of all their friends smelling like whiskey and puke."

"What does that have to do with the guy?"

"I lied to him too. I lied about my life, about Francesca. Now he'll never speak to me ever again. I should have never started lying.

My parents blame everything on you, maybe I should blame you for my problems too. I started this whole lying thing when Francesca would stay out all night with you, then sneak into the house right before the sun came up. I should have told my parents I was worried about Francesca."

Donny's eyes open a little more. "You honestly think they were clueless? C'mon."

"Yeah, but you said at the bar, I was the only one who knew Francesca was in trouble and didn't do anything about it."

"I was drunk and angry. I was pissed and wanted to blame somebody. I got tired of blaming myself."

"What about Francesca shielding me from the truth?"

"That part was true. So stop carrying the load. Stop thinking people are perfect and life is perfect. Lower your expectations."

Donny takes a deep breath. "Go home and fix what's broken. You go tell that guy you love the truth. Every truth you can think of, tell him. Make a grand entrance, give it all you got, sis. You have to try. Don't stay here and hide. Nothin' good comes out of hiding. Take it from me."

Donny lets out a huge breath. His eyes are closed. He starts snoring.

"Donny."

He doesn't answer. He's completely out. I walk over close and stare at his stomach to make sure he's still breathing.

"I'll call you in a few days," I whisper.

Donny's arms are folded across his chest. His eyebrows are wrinkled up like he's in pain. He doesn't answer.

I sit back down on the edge of the bed. The TV's on super low, some lame adult cartoon show playing on the cable comedy channel. I sit and stare at the glow of characters yelling swears at each other.

I'm sure the dirty brown and orange bedspread with flowers used to be pretty and cheerful, but now they've lost their color, their life. Even the faucet in the bathroom is broken—I can hear it dripping.

I look back at Donny, his face all leathery and white, his hair is all greasy. I decide to write him a note. Maybe when he wakes up, he'll want someone to talk to, to help him get back on track. I fish through my purse and find a receipt from Target and write three sentences.

Donny,

I promise to fix my life if you promise to fix yours. We could help each other.

Love, Mello

I reach into my purse. I've been carrying the potbelly stove magnet around since I took it off the fridge when we were packing up Francesca's stuff.

I put the magnet on top of the note on the nightstand next to Donny and walk out.

Chapter 20

What love means

1. Risk.
2. Being honest with yourself and the person you love.
3. Accepting someone for who they are.
4. Courage to reveal your true self to people.
5. Total truth.

I told Dad on the way home what Donny said to do. He agreed to let me take the car for one hour and go talk to Howie. So I went straight to the party store and bought the biggest red heart I could find. I had to walk sideways through the door. Then I went to the florist.

The snow is thick, but not heavy enough to affect the roads in any real way. It's February, and at this point all the drivers in Chicago are more used to driving on snow than on dry pavement. I've texted Howie ten times and I've left him ten messages to please let me talk to him. He's in total avoidance mode.

I drive to the ice rink first, hoping he's here. I don't want to go to his house and possibly face his parents.

Howie's car isn't anywhere in the lot, but I go in anyhow. He could have gotten a ride with his cousin.

I walk over to the benches where Howie's locker is. Nikki's lacing up her skates. She grunts.

"Hi, Nikki."

"Hi."

"You know where Howie is?"

"Not sure, why?"

"I need to talk to him."

"You two get into a fight?"

"No, yeah, well, sort of."

Nikki eyes me up and down. "He's my closest guy friend and I don't want to see him get screwed."

"I totally need to talk to him right away. He won't answer my calls or texts. Can you help me?"

"Not sure." She gets up off the bench, turns around and opens her locker. She pulls her phone out and punches in a text. I assume she's texting Howie. She taps her finger on her phone. "I gotta be on the ice in a minute. If he doesn't get back to me—" Her phone chimes. "I guess he's home. He says he's already done skating, which means he cut his practice short for today."

"Thanks. I owe you."

"You better not hurt him."

***

I park on Howie's driveway and send him a text that I'm out here and need to talk. I text him again and again. I tell him I'm sitting in his driveway freezing and I'm not going to leave until he lets me in.

I sit out in my car, with the heater going, for ten minutes. I text him over and over.

Finally, he opens the front door. I get out of the car, with my guitar, a heart the size of an elephant's head and the three-dozen white roses. My purse falls off my shoulder as I walk up the steps.

Howie's arms are crossed against his chest as he steps out onto his front stoop. The giant heart slips down to my knees.

"I'm not making any promises by letting you in." He takes my guitar from me and closes the door.

I'm totally covered in snow, my shoes, my hair, the roses. Flakes are stuck to my eyelashes. "Can we go somewhere private?"

"My parents aren't home. They're gone till seven-ish."

"You want to talk right here?"

"Why not?" He puts the guitar down and crosses his arms.

"Wow. You're kind of a dickhead when you're mad, aren't you?"

Howie tilts his head. "Nice. Wow, you're totally winning me over right now."

"You're right, strike that from the record. Let me start over. Sorry, I'm a little worked up." I roll my eyes.

"Ah, yeah."

"Um, here." I hand him the flowers. "These are for you. I chose white because they're the color of the ice."

"Thanks."

I'm about to hand him the giant heart too, but think I'm going a little over the top, so I set the heart down.

My coat's all wet and heavy and I can't move my arms enough to play my guitar. "I need to take my coat off."

"Go ahead." He holds the flowers, still with his arms folded.

I take my coat off and lay it down on the rug in front of the door. Snow falls off my bangs. I go to pick up my guitar and glance over at Howie. He's standing tall, his arms crossed like he's checked out. He's not even here. No matter what I do at this point he won't care. He's totally made up his mind.

I won't play for him, I can't play for him like this.

I look at my guitar in the case and mumble under my breath, "Forget it."

"What?" he says.

I turn back around to face Howie. I want to tell him how pissed I am. I was so sure the roses and the ginormous heart would prove to him how much he means to me. And I thought if he saw me carrying my guitar I've been terrified of touching or going near since my sister died, he'd totally crack. I imagined he'd run up to me and hug me and tell me everything is okay, but obviously that's not gonna happen. This was a mistake.

"Sorry I interrupted your life," I say.

"Fine."

"Fine."

I put my wet coat back on. I bet this is how Francesca felt. I bet her hurt was so bad inside she couldn't find a reason to fight, couldn't find a reason to let people in.

I open the door.

"Wait," he says. "That's it?"

I turn around. "What do you care?"

"Seeing you here, all covered in snow and wearing your black coat, carrying your guitar, I think you came here for a reason and I want to hear what you have to say."

The back of my throat closes up. I turn around. "You want me to stand here and beg, tell you I'm totally screwed up and don't have a clue how to live my life without lying, or I never meant to hurt people and I don't know how or why I started lying? I'll tell you how I think I started lying. Once you get burned, you learn how painful fire can be, so you pull your hand away without even thinking, right? But once you burn your finger super bad, you pull it away even when your finger feels the slightest little bit of heat. I got tired of getting burned, get it?"

Howie looks confused. "Sort of."

"That didn't make sense?"

"Not really. I didn't get the whole thing, but I think I get you."

"You do."

"Yeah," he says.

"I need you to believe me, I'm telling the truth about France. My parents said no, but when this stomach thing happened, they decided I should get away from here and were going to surprise me at my birthday party with the news."

"Serious?"

"Yeah."

"So you're going?" he asks.

"Yeah." I close my eyes. "But you'll be the first person I'll miss."

I think about what Donny told me, to put everything I got into this.

I open my eyes. "If we were to start dating again, I want you to believe me when I tell you it will tear me up inside to leave you, but I promise I'll text or call or Skype or whatever every day."

"Every day?" he asks.

I nod. "And one more thing I want to come clean about." I can't look Howie in the eye, so I look down at his feet. "My sister died accidentally, but it wasn't a car accident." I look up at him. "She died of a drug overdose."

"Was she an addict?"

"No, I mean, I don't know, maybe. And if we're gonna be honest with each other, I hate it when people say that about her, like she had a choice. Something ate her alive, like an alien in a monster movie. People don't understand. No one blames people who have cancer. Why should they blame a person for having an addiction problem?"

"Because people who get cancer don't have a choice."

"That's what everybody thinks. Truth is, sometimes there is no choice. Sometimes the addiction takes over and wins. That's why people die."

"How do you know for sure what happened to your sister was an accident?" he asks.

"Because she told me she was scared of dying. She wanted to go to an AA meeting, she wanted me to take her, but I didn't. I thought we could go the next day." My hands are in fists and I can hardly breathe. "I thought there was time. I didn't do the right thing."

"Carmella, it's not your fault."

"I know, but sometimes I still think I could have done something." My voice echoes up through the two-story staircase.

"If you keep thinking like that, you're going to end up crazy like my parents."

I think about what Donny said about being totally honest. "Sometimes I wonder if I'm halfway there."

Howie grabs me. He holds me tight and whispers in my ear. "I'm sorry. Why didn't you tell me?"

I whisper back. "I didn't tell anyone."

Howie and I hold onto each other for a freakishly long time. And then he kisses me and I kiss him back.

"You know what you need? You need to skate more," he says.

"You think so?" I smile.

"Yep. How about as soon as the stomach thing heals? I think you have a future as an amateur once a week ice skater."

"Okay. So you'll be, like, my coach?"

"Yeah," Howie says. "I smell cigarette smoke. Do you?"

"Yeah, I do."

Howie sniffs my neck. "You don't smoke."

"No, but my sister did." I smile.

Some Statistics

- Drug overdose death rates have risen steadily in the United States since 1970.

- Accidental overdose death rates have increased roughly five-fold since 1990.

- In 2006, 26,400 unintentional drug overdose deaths occurred in the United States.

- Drug overdose deaths were second only to motor vehicle crash deaths among leading causes of unintentional injury death in 2006, according to Centers for Disease Control.

All information provided by the Centers for Disease Control and Prevention. *www.cdc.gov*

Acknowledgments

In the basement of my parents' house in 2005, my brother Bill and my husband Ed, talked me into pursuing my dream. None of us understood the magnitude or scope of dedication, blood, sweat and tears it takes to learn the craft of fiction writing, but sometimes being ignorant is a good thing. Without their conviction and constant support and encouragement, I would not be an author; a dream I kept buried in my soul since I was twelve years old. I owe them both – big time, but I must give an extra-special thanks to my husband, Ed. He has made sacrifices for me, stood by me, but most importantly, he was the ultimate cheerleader. He is a true partner in life, love and the pursuit of happiness.

My journey in becoming a novelist would not be possible without my parents. They gave me the values, morals and work ethic necessary to becoming a fiction writer. My parents are the pillars of strength in our family and I'm proud to be their daughter. My mother never doubted me and encouraged me to keep going every step of the way. She's made countless dinners for me and my family when I've been too busy writing to cook. She taught me to put one hundred percent effort into everything I do and to always follow my gut instincts. I'm grateful for her invaluable life lessons. And I thank my father who taught me to never give up and keep fighting. He's available to help out whenever I'm in need and has pretty much been on call since my kids were born. I'm so grateful to have a dad I can call my wingman.

My son and my daughter deserve special recognition for being the best kids out there, especially in the last two years. They have become independent, mature and resourceful and always understand when the writing comes before them. I also thank them for always providing honest immediate feedback. Back in the beginning stages of learning the craft, they were brutal in letting me know when something truly sucked. Conversely, when they tell me I'm the best writer in the world now, I believe them. And, they give the best hugs too. Priceless support I cannot live without.

My writing journey went from a slow throttle to full speed ahead when I was accepted into the University of Chicago Creative Writing program. Stephanie Friedman, Achy Obejas, Bayo Ojikutu, Ben Lytal and Dina Elenbogen saw potential in my words and because of their belief in me, I am able to realize my dream. I must make special mention to Gary Wilson, my mentor. Writing fiction is an incredibly intense, difficult craft and even more difficult to teach, but Gary has mastered both. He changed my life and I will forever be grateful.

I am also eternally grateful to my fellow comrades at the University of Chicago. Words cannot express what they mean to me. I feel so lucky to have had such awesome people walk along side me in this journey. Karen Anderson, David Ben-Aire, Rachel Farrell, Ralph Gerbie, Maureen Hartigan, Kathy Neumeyer, Fred Sherwood and Sophia Tareen are all brilliant writers who I will always admire. I enjoyed every minute of our time together and hope we continue to share our journeys together.

There are more comrades who were with me at the very beginning stages of my journey. Without the help of Off Campus

Writer's Workshop in Winnetka, becoming an author would not have been possible. The entire group of writers who meet every Thursday morning helped give me the confidence and conviction to keep moving forward. They are the best and I'd like to give particular thanks to Susan Bearman, Ardis Berghoff, Carole Cotter, Victoria Cunha, the late Nancy Crabb, Dick Davidson, Mary Driver, Hellen Gallagher, Almira Studillo Gilles, Karen Gray-Keeler, Susan Lutz Kenyon, Kathy Gregg, Ellen Mc Knight, Jeanne Monty, Patricia J. Murphy, Beverly Patt, Becky Redfield, Brenda Rossini, Sue Roupp, Gay Scheffen, Mary Beth Schewitz. Ruth Spiro, Harriet Clare Wadeson and Cate Wallace. And a very special thank you goes out to Mr. Fred Shafer, literary editor, writer, workshop leader and lecturer in creative writing at Northwestern University. He believed in me way before I believed in myself.

Publishing a book takes a team and I'm thrilled to give tribute to the people who worked with me on this project. Alison Dasho is a truly gifted editor who did an outstanding job with all the edits in this book and will go down in history as my first editor. Dale Pease collaborated with me in designing the cover and did the best job ever. Diana Cox did an amazingly fast proofread for me. Cheryl Perez formatted the book and put up with my silly questions and timing issues like a pro. And thanks to Tony Bondick for your technical assistance and emotional support.

A special shout out goes to special friends, who are like family to me. First, thanks to the whole Kurpiewski family for all your love and support, especially Chris. Without you, I would never know what true friendship means. And thank you Scottie, not only for your endless support and friendship, but for being partially responsible for my third nickname, which I will always cherish. And I must thank the old dinner group, Laura and Eric Goff and Stacey and James

Stiles. I can always count on you to be there when I need to laugh at myself and at life. You have stuck by me through all the good and the bad. And finally, I'm sending a big giant virtual hug to my BFF from first grade, who can still make me laugh until I pee on myself and should get a special award for listening to my big pie-in-the-sky-dreams since I was six. Thank you Mary Jane O'Brien Rich. Blood sisters for life, for sure.

I'd love to list all the other vital people in my life, my friends, neighbors and extended family who stood by me and supported me in every which way possible. But if I listed all of you (you know who you are) and all that you've done for me, it would encompass another novel-length piece of work. To all of you who believed, who supported, who encouraged and who stood by me, thank you.

About the Author

Shari A. Brady is a native Chicagoan and previously had so many careers she's lost count. A graduate of Loyola University's Business School and University of Chicago's Creative Writing program, she's finally a full-time writer, a dream she's carried with her since she was twelve. She lives in suburban Chicago with her awesome husband, two of the best kids ever, and their shelter dog, Betty Queen Elizabeth. This is her first novel and her last career.

A portion of the proceeds from this book will be donated to the FAIR Foundation to support its mission of helping provide financial assistance to families of addicted teens, who cannot afford the cost of substance abuse treatment so they can get life-saving, family-healing care. For more information visit the FAIR Foundation website @ www.thefairfoundation.org

If you'd like to make a donation, please visit my website at www.sharibrady.com and click on the OMNI youth button.

17069976R00146

Made in the USA
Charleston, SC
25 January 2013